Millionaire
in
Flip Flops

Millionaire in Flip Flops

The Lifestyle Edition

By
Sue Cooper

Editor and Writing Coach
Cricket Desmarais

Dog House Publishing
Key West, Florida

ISBN-13: 978-0-9860308-8-8
ISBN-10: 0-9860308-8-0

Cover and back photos by Peter Green at
www.PeterGreenPhoto.com
Interior design and layout by Scott McCollum

For more information visit www.MillionaireInFlipFlops.com

Printed in the United States of America.

To my parents,
Rich and Veronica Cooper
Aka "Veronirich"
*Your unconditional love
and support have always made me
feel like I could do anything.*

CONTENTS

WARNING

Before you begin this book, I want to warn you. Once you set your plans in motion and start to truly experience your life you will never settle for going back to your old life again. You will constantly crave more, do more, think more, and feel more alive.

If you do happen to fall back to your old ways, you may even find yourself more bored than you were before, and possibly disappointed in yourself, too, knowing that a whole new world is knocking at your door and you are choosing not to open it.

So what are you going to do?

Obviously, you picked up this book, which means you are eager for some sort of change. Change requires a willingness to move forward, along with a commitment to try new things and see things from a different perspective.

You could do nothing. Stop here, now. The choice is yours. As a Millionaire in Flip Flops, I'm here to tell you that opening the door will be more than worth it.

PRELUDE

THE FISHERMAN

An American tourist was at the pier of a small coastal Mexican village when a small boat with just one fisherman docked. Inside the small boat were several large yellowfin tuna. The tourist complimented the Mexican on the quality of his fish and asked how long it took to catch them.

The Mexican replied, "Only a little while."

The tourist then asked, "Why didn't you stay out longer and catch more fish?"

The Mexican said, "With this I have more than enough to support my family's needs."

The tourist then asked, "But what do you do with the rest of your time?"

The Mexican fisherman said, "I sleep late, fish a little, play with my children, take a siesta with my wife, Maria, stroll into the village each evening where I sip wine and play guitar with my amigos. I have a full and busy life."

The tourist scoffed, "I can help you. You should spend more time fishing, and with the proceeds, buy a bigger boat. With the proceeds from the bigger boat you could buy several boats. Eventually you would have a fleet of fishing boats. Instead of selling your catch to a middleman you would sell directly to the processor, eventually opening your own cannery. You would control the product, processing and distribution. You could leave this small coastal fishing village and move to Mexico City, then Los Angeles and eventually New York where you could run your ever-expanding enterprise."

The Mexican fisherman asked, "But how long will this all take?"

The tourist replied, "Fifteen to twenty years."

"But what then?" asked the Mexican.

The tourist laughed and said, "That's the best part. When the time is right you would sell your company stock to the public and become very rich. You would make millions."

"Millions?...Then what?"

The American said, "Then you would retire. Move to a small coastal fishing village where you would sleep late, fish a little, play with your kids, take siestas with your wife, stroll to the village in the evenings where you could sip wine and play your guitar with your amigos."

INTRODUCTION
WHAT IT REALLY MEANS TO BE A MILLIONAIRE

I live a pretty simple life. I live on an island, have my own business where I work with my closest friends and am surrounded by great friends who feel like family. My dog comes with me everywhere. My work is an extension of my lifestyle, which is also simple but incredibly fulfilling.

Every day I have people tell me that I have the greatest job or that I am so lucky to live this life. My response is a resounding, "Yes! I am lucky!" I think it's also important to mention that I actually created this lifestyle. We all have the power within us to create the life we truly want to live. Although not a writer by trade, I decided to share the stories, advice, lessons and adventures in my life as a Millionaire in Flip Flops.

If you're reading this book to find out how to make a million bucks, you might want to stop here and reconsider. This book is not necessarily about stacking up enough cash to make you a bona-fide millionaire, though my guess is that if you are truly following your life's path with a sense of tenacity, wisdom and heart, you likely could.

What Millionaire in Flip Flops **will** do is take you through the journey of creating the lifestyle of a Millionaire in Flip Flops, where you do what you want, when you want, and hopefully how and with whom you want. All you need is an open mind, some courage, a little creativity and a willingness to let it all hang out. Refer back to the fisherman story if you feel stumped about what I am saying.

Ultimately, I hope this book will nudge you towards falling in love with your life so that you will succeed in being happy, the richest gift of all. I hope that it will help you see that true success is actually a lifestyle, or more specifically, the lifestyle **you** want to create.

In the chapters ahead there are thought-provoking exercises. A pen and a journal are pretty helpful.

Most of Americans spend a majority of their day working hard doing something they don't like, sometimes for thirty years or more, only to "retire" to a part time job. In fact, Forbes.com did a survey showing 71% of Americans don't like their job. Wow! What a way to spend a third of every day.

Most will tell you their life isn't working for them. More typically, they are working just to keep alive. Unfortunately, so many of us follow along in that mainstream, allowing that standard way of living to be part of our own. Work becomes one defined part of life and play another. This sense of dis-integration does just that: it erodes our sense of self and deteriorates our sense of hope and our ability to dream along the way.

The stories in this book will take you through my personal journey and quest to let go of the corporate job that fit me like a bad pair of shoes to find a better way of living, ultimately landing me the position as owner of Lazy Dog Adventures, an outdoor adventure outfit in Key West, Florida. How, you wonder? By merging all aspects of my life, work, play, family, friends, spirituality, fitness and health to create a truly organic lifestyle. When it comes down to it, organic is not just the way you eat. It's also a way of life.

This book will give you tips on how to better enjoy your life by letting go of what you are "supposed to do" and embrace life and all of its ups and downs. We are here to live not just survive! Jump in, now! Don't wait 'til Monday to start. Experience your life the way you see fit and don't worry about the outcome. Shake things up and give yourself permission to live outside your comfort zone for a while. See what happens. I promise you that by doing so you will grow.

CHAPTER ONE

WAKE-UP CALL

Open your eyes, look within.
Are you satisfied with the life you're living?
-Bob Marley

As the owner of a kayak and paddleboard outfit on a sub-tropical island, I meet lots of people from around the world, many of whom like to share their stories and hear mine. I am amazed at how many of them hate their job and where they live. Why do people put themselves through this? Do people think that because it is a "job" they are not supposed to enjoy themselves? Why do people live where the temperature drops to ten degrees when they hate the cold or live in the humid south and hate sweating? These are things people can control and yet they often do nothing about. They just muddle though another work week.

I believe your job should be an extension of your life, your values, and your beliefs. Why be one person at work and another at home? We spend so much time at work that we'd better find a way to enjoy it, or find another job altogether. Life isn't about making a living, it's about living a life. I went on vacation to visit my parents who had retired in Florida. They had a beautiful house with a pool, lived on the golf course and were always out whenever I would call. They were like teenagers having a great time. When I showed up at their house, it was packed with people. They were having a barbeque and pool party. I started talking to one of the guests as I watched this great energy circle amid a truly fun group of people.

"You all sure look like you are having fun," I said to my parents' friend.

He responded, "We are all retired. This is the **real** us," he added, putting emphasis on the word "real." For me, that was the kicker that not only got me thinking, but helped pave the way for the choices I would soon be making.

"For the last thirty years we were all someone else."

I saw these people were all having a great time and life was treating them well now. I didn't want to be someone else for thirty years. I didn't want to pretend to be someone I wasn't. I didn't want to be someone else's version of "successful." In my book, part of being successful means being who you are.

At that point in my life, I was working for a major shoe corporation, had high accolades from my "superiors" and was making great money. However, things were starting to change for me. I didn't want to play office politics, I didn't want to dress up for work and traffic was too much. I wanted a career to fit my lifestyle. I wanted to enjoy every day of work and not wait thirty years for it to happen.

Ironically, I had been brought into my boss' office numerous times: I n e e d e d t o dress more professionally and wear heels. I guess my angels were throwing me signs, even way back then to get on with living my life the way I saw fit. The bottom line was this: I wanted to wear flip flops to work!

Like so many who are attracted to the idea of success (typically represented by large sums of money and loads of material things), it was a bit of a transition to seal my new thinking process and my perspectives on what true success actually meant. The fisherman story came along at precisely the right time, proving to be a perfect catalyst to put me on my path and take me away from everything I thought I wanted. When I read that small but powerful parable, I realized that success was a lifestyle and I wanted to be in charge of how it was created.

Think back to the story of the Mexican fisherman, for he illustrates a very fine point we'd all be wise to understand. Some millionaires don't have the time to live like a millionaire. They work eighty plus hours a week, leaving little "free" time except maybe a few weeks of holiday. Yes, they may have great toys that money can buy, but if I could only pass on one lesson to you it would be this: life is about doing, not having. Toys are fun, and yes, even vacations are fun, but what if you could do what you wanted to do, every day? What if your work merged to become the lifestyle you dream of?

WHO REALLY LIVES LIKE A MILLIONAIRE?

This is a peek into the week of two people living very different lives.

#1
Worked eighty hours.
Worked through lunch hour.
Ordered take-out five nights because of exhaustion.
Slept most of the weekend because of exhaustion.
Didn't see friends or family as much as preferred.

#2
Went fishing for dinner. Cooked up a great recipe for friends.
Went boating with friends and dogs.
Grilled out at a friend's house.
Sunbathed by the pool with friends.
Went to a hotel hot tub, had a drink and soaked with friends.
Ran five days, totaling twenty-five miles.
Swam laps in the ocean.
Took dog to work outside by the water.
Rode a bike to work.

Worked on a laptop outside at the work picnic table.
Dressed up for a costume party, danced and stayed out until 3 am having fun with friends.
Did yoga under the stars on the beach.
Watched the sun set into the ocean, again and again and again.
Took boat out to check stone crab traps.
Paddleboarded.

Now here's the kicker: Person #1 is a millionaire, lives in Connecticut and commutes to New York City. Person #2 makes forty-thousand a year and lives in Key West. Who really is the "millionaire" here? Which would you prefer?

We all have to make a living, but how will you use your time to make a life?

DO THIS:
Make a List of What You Do In a Week

What do you do for work? What do you do with your free time? What are your hobbies? (Do they involve doing, or do they involve having?) What, if any, type of weekly exercise do you do? Do you cook for yourself or others or do you eat out?

Go though your entire week and list what you do. Then list how much you make. This is a good reference point for you to look back on once you put your plan into motion.

WHAT DRIVES YOU?

A friend and I were sitting together over tea one day when she asked, "What drives you?" But she didn't stop there, she asked many other questions, too. "What was it that drove you to leave your job and move to an island? What drove you to open a business? What drove you to paddleboard race?"

I hadn't ever really thought about these things because drive is something I have always naturally had. But looking back, I can say there are a few things that drive me. I believe:

- When things aren't working for you, change them!
- Life is not about getting by or settling. It's about living.
- I want to do everything because I can.
- I don't want to limit myself by only what I know now, so I need to do everything to see what else is out there.

This idea of **living** is something I want to stress. Think of some of your most favorite times: a place where you vacationed, an amazing adventure you had, fun times with friends. Don't just read these words. Stop for a minute and really think about them. Let the memories of them come back on the big picture screen of your mind.

Now, when you think of these times, do they seem squashed in between your life of working? For many of us, that's probably true. Imagine if these memories weren't just fun times tucked into your life of work. Imagine such things as part of your daily life.

It's my hope to teach you how to integrate what matters most to you and help you discover what motivates you, what inspires you and brings you true happiness so that you feel your life as something fully lived.

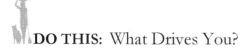**DO THIS:** What Drives You?

What are some key phrases you live by? Write them down, quick, now. It's ok to admit if some of them aren't exactly your best cheerleaders. In fact, if you are honest, you'll see what sorts of mantras you've made that are helping, or not helping, to shape your life.

MY STORY

Something that has always driven me is athletics and the idea that I might one day be a professional athlete. At 21, I had different ideas of what this would be like than what actually happened. I was totally and utterly dedicated to running back then, and my sights were set on marathons and the Olympics. Little did I know that two decades later I would be a professional paddleboard racer, traveling the circuit whenever possible, having a blast while also promoting my outdoor adventure company Lazy Dog, based in Key West, Florida. Back then, I hadn't even heard of paddleboarding.

I decided to travel, to live in England with relatives and train for the London Marathon with hopes of qualifying for the Olympic Trials. It had always been my dream, so I was going for it. I had to run a two hour and 45 minute marathon to qualify. My best had been a three hour and four minute marathon I ran in New Jersey when I was in college. I knew I didn't have the body of a marathoner to be among the elite runners, but I did have a chance to qualify. It was a long shot, but I was up for the challenge.

I hung out with all the guys I ran with. We would go on incredible runs throughout the countryside, twenty miles of just fields and hills. I experienced runner's high on a daily basis. I imagine it is what it's like to find spirituality in mediation. To this day my runs are my way of meditating. After a winter in England, I ran the London Marathon in April and ran it in two hours and 58 minutes. I was excited that I ran my best time but disappointed that I missed qualifying by only thirteen minutes.

Yet the experience was the beginning of my new adventures and a change of mindset in life--that there are no failures, only experiences. In fact, if there is such thing as failure, it is not to try and not succeed, but to do nothing at all. If you go for your goal and you "fail," it gives you the opportunity to close the door and move on, creating more space in your mind and heart for other things in life. If you never try you will always wonder "what if?". I can pretty much guarantee that you will regret it later on in life.

I had tried and it was a hell of an experience: from grueling workouts where I could hardly walk the next day and had to have a masseuse come in and massage my calves just so I could get out and run the next day, to great new friendships, getting to know my grandparents, living in another country and trying my best. It was now time to shut the door and open another. I had no idea what door I would be opening other than returning to the States.

With these things in mind, I came back from England and worked at a sporting goods store in town. I wanted to be around sports but had a business mind. My work ethic came from my self-motivation and dedication to training, so I quickly became assistant manager of the store. I would travel around the state on the weekends running races and making more money in the race than my weekly paycheck from the sports store. I did this for the next few years. Then I got bored.

My life of racing on the weekends and working retail at a sports shoe store left me uninspired. I decided to try and get a job at an international shoe corporation that had just moved its headquarters out of New York City into the town where I currently worked. I had turned down an offer from IBM a few years earlier and I felt like I needed to give the idea of the corporate lifestyle a chance.

I got the interview. Though I lacked traditional experience, I was determined and highly self-motivated, and told my interviewer that what I lacked in experience I would make up in work ethic, and that I would become one of his best employees. I got the job and was hired for an entry-level customer service position. I was to start my new corporate job two weeks later.

When I woke up the next morning there was an article in the paper that advertised a professional women's baseball league that was starting and they were having open tryouts at West Point that weekend. I am a baseball-aholic. I love the game, studying the stats, the chess-like tactical approach to the game. I was always a good athlete; while I only played softball up until ninth grade, I could throw a damn ball like no one. I decided to try out.

My sister and I went to the parking lot of a corporate office after hours and threw the baseball around. It was the middle of winter, ice was everywhere and we were freezing, but I was excited about the opportunity. I went to the batting cages and practiced.

That Saturday I drove two hours in a snow storm to West Point for tryouts by myself. I was intimidated but my adrenaline was pumping. The first part of the day was filled with all athletic tests: an obstacle course, 50 meter dash, agility tests. I could run forever, but I have never been the fastest short distance runner. I wasn't feeling all that confident until I looked around on the start line and noticed the size of the women I was racing against. No problem. I outran almost all of them.

The team scouts were going to pick sixty women to make it to the next day, then pick thirty who would be invited to Colorado Springs for tryouts, along with thirty women from six other cities that were hosting tryouts to then be narrowed down to a team of twenty-five. It was a long shot for sure, but at the end of the day one I was in the top group.

I braved the icy conditions and came up again the next day. Now it was technical. I tried out for third base even though I had always been a short stop. I didn't have as strong of an arm as the other girls but I hung in. Batting practice, fielding, pitching--everyone had to be tested at each station. At the end of the day, I felt good.

We waited on the inside bleachers for our names to be called. They decided that some were going to be sent home and others would be notified by mail. They began naming names of those who were cut. Tears were shed, loud cries by one whose father was there in his coach's uniform, comforting his daughter and eyeing the scouts as if to say "you guys don't know what a talent you just passed on." It was amazing how upset people became. Then, the day was over, and my name hadn't been called. I made it through to the "notified by mail" group.

The day before I started my new job, a job I was very excited about, I received a letter from the Colorado Bullets. Before I opened the letter, I asked myself what I would do if I made it. It was a once-in-a-lifetime opportunity; I couldn't give that up for a job that would be there when I got back. And even if this company decided not to take me back, others would. I opened the letter. "We are sorry to inform you…."

The next day I began my corporate adventure. I had no regrets and yet another incredible experience to add to my life. Unlike the girl who cried when told she didn't make it and probably

15

saw failure, I just saw experience. I came close to not trying out because what if I made the team and also had this new job? I didn't want to ever wonder "what if" so I did it and let the cards fall where they may.

I started my customer service job, ready for my first dabble into the corporate world. I was so excited I came in early and stayed late. After a few months, I worked into a new position as a "tech rep"- a position that I created with my favorite company executive, Craig. I traveled around the country visiting stores that sold our shoes and held clinics for the sales staff so they could better sell our products. I flew all over the country, made my own schedule, and developed the position as I saw fit. I was working all the time and loving it, except when I traveled on weekends for work and missed my soccer games or a party. I loved work but didn't want it to get in the way of my social life.

While I was working like crazy, everyone around me, or should I say above me in the corporate ladder, was being fired and no one was being hired in their place. I was taking on more and more responsibility at work and loving it. What a great opportunity I was given. Interestingly, despite the growth of my job and job requirements, my title was still "tech rep," which was still a low-level position.

Our company had nine divisions around the country and ours was lucky (or unlucky) to also house the CEO, CFO and board members. The CEO was always involved in our division, yelling and telling people what to do. I was still young and had respect for my elders, so I tried to soak it all in, learn from the top dog. At one point, I was approached by a colleague informing me that I was to attend the next executive conference, a gathering of top dogs from all divisions. Since I wasn't an executive I was a bit confused but figured they needed help organizing the event.

16

A month later, as I sat at a table in a conference room full of executives I didn't know, my name was called. I was nominated as "Executive of the Year" by my work colleagues. It was an incredible moment, one of such pride and accomplishment. The best part was that I had been voted for by my work colleagues, an acknowledgement I will take with me throughout my life. There I was with an entry level job, selected as the "Executive of the Year." The next day I was the Executive Director of Marketing and Advertising with a 35% raise. Life was treating me well until a month later, when out of nowhere, my two-year relationship crumbled.

Looking back, I'm not surprised. I spent more time, energy and mental thought on work than my relationship. I loved my job and thought my relationship would always be there. When we broke up, I was heartbroken. I struggled to focus at work. I was sad and not fun to be around.

I went on a business trip to Los Angeles, and as I always do when I enter the hotel room, I put on the television for noise There on the television was a man I became convinced was talking directly to me. "Are you unmotivated in life? Do you want more from life?" I sat on the bed and watched the entire thirty minute infomercial and at the end of it, I ordered the $180, twenty-eight day tape set by inspirational speaker Tony Robbins. When I got back from my trip my tapes were waiting for me.

With a tape a day for twenty eight days, I couldn't get enough. I was doubling up to do as many as I could, working in the workbook journal that came with the set. I was so sick and tired of complaining about how sad and upset I was over my relationship ending that I was going to do everything and anything I could to get myself out of this state. I read books, I went out and met new people, became quarterback of a state flag football team (which I never had played before), tried out for and made a semi-pro soccer team, worked out every day, and listened to my tapes. The tapes helped motivate me. One small change let to another, and

17

then another, and the next thing I knew I had a new energy about myself.

In a matter of a month, before I had finished the tapes, I was finding out who I was and what I wanted in life. I became very comfortable with being alone, which I had never been. It's a place of great confidence and peacefulness. It doesn't mean you have to be alone, just be comfortable alone. I didn't need anyone else to make me happy but myself. A few months later my partner and I got back together. She said I had become the happy and fun person that she had fallen in love with two years earlier.

I continued excelling at work but I soon noticed things weren't what I thought they were. The CEO would tear people apart in front of everyone at the office. He would say one thing, then do another. He would trash our huge marketing plans, take us to his school of marketing by treating us to his lessons in a derogatory way. We would then change our marketing plan only for him to trash it again and go back to the original one.

Where in the past I tried to learn all I could because I thought his way was the right way or "corporate way," I now felt he was, well, basically a jerk. He was disrespectful, unkind and flaky, offering no clear idea of what he really wanted other than to hear himself speak.

One day during his "schooling" at our marketing meeting something hit me. The CEO was yelling at all of us, and right there around the oval conference room table I began to have my "a-ha! moment." I couldn't hear him anymore, instead hearing my own inner wisdom. "Why am I putting up with this jerk? I have soaked up all I can and don't need this anymore."

And by the way, what I learned from him was what NOT to do, many lessons I would take into my future employment. In this state of bliss I had a huge realization: I don't want to do this anymore. The voice of my inner wisdom took over. "If this is corporate, I don't want it. If I have to pretend I like this guy to move up the ladder, I don't want to. If I have to show this moron respect, I can't. This is not the way to deal with people. The only way I can work in this environment is to change my morals and values and nobody can make me do that."

As I sat there realizing this wasn't for me and how his actions compromised who I was, a tear came down my cheek. Of course he saw it. He jumped on me so fast and tore me down, trying to make an example out of me, with complete disrespect. I stayed in my moment silently, still barely able to hear him because I was tuning him out. He was nothing to me anymore, not even worth a catty remark. I actually felt sorry for him.

What he didn't know was that my tear was not from being upset about the verbal lashing, it was a tear from the realization that I couldn't go on with this any longer. My growth was exceeding the limitations I was being presented with and compromising my values. It was time for bigger and better things.

Although I didn't know what these bigger and better things were, a few days later I shocked myself and my fellow employees and resigned. A few months later I moved to Key West, the warmest place on the map I could find in the United States. Just about all of my fellow former co-workers thought I was crazy but also wished they were doing the same.

I can't tell you how many times I heard, "I wish I could do that," a phrase I still hear almost daily today. And my answer is still the same today as it was then: You can.

DO THIS: Your A-ha! Moment

Can you pinpoint the moment you received your wake-up call? Or maybe you've had several, and just haven't really answered it yet?

Write them down, quick, and read them. You'll answer them soon enough for sure.

CHAPTER TWO

BREAKING OUT OF THE NORM

Do not go where the path may lead,
Go instead where there is no path
and leave a trail.
-Ralph Waldo Emerson

Growing up, I always tried to fit into the mainstream, to go with the flow and stick with the masses. It was always a struggle. I battled the divided feeling I'd get from doing what everyone else was doing and not doing what I felt in my heart.

It wasn't really an unhappy time, but it was confusing. I knew from my parents and their lead-by-example-life that I could keep in the mainstream *and* explore my options without great discord among my friends and family. Things were always mostly going well but were not perfect. Something was always missing.

I was born in England and at the age of three, my dad got a job with IBM and moved the family to Darien, Connecticut, a very conservative wealthy town just outside of New York City. It was a great place to grow up as a child- safe, small, and near the water. My dad worked and my mom took care of my older brother John, my sister Julie and me. It was here where the framework of my Millionaire in Flip Fops lifestyle was created.

Our family didn't have the biggest house or the nicest cars. My parents lived within their means. They wanted us to always have the money for adventures. Whether it was traveling across the county for three weeks in a station wagon or going to an action park, we were able to do it. It was all about adventures and experiences, not about what we had.

I was very shy and a momma's girl, not wanting anyone but her to hold me. I also had a British accent, which made other people harass me and say that I spoke funny. There were two girls in my class, Leslie and Catherine, who bullied me constantly. They made so much fun of how I spoke that I would never speak up in class. Even when they weren't in my class anymore (I stayed back in fourth grade), I was so afraid of being teased that I never spoke.

Years later, in tenth grade, we had to do a five minute speech in English class. I told the teacher I would not be doing it. He tried everything, telling me I could talk about anything I wanted, even an apple, anything just to get me to participate. I refused and took an "F" for the quarter. When a teacher would ask a question I would never look up. I figured if I didn't look at the teacher the teacher wouldn't look at me and ask me for the answer.

My mom's early years in the States were much different than mine. Though she didn't know anyone, she joined a town tennis group, learned how to play and quickly made a bunch of lifelong friends and became the town tennis champion for years to come. I love my mom. She has led her life by example and little did I know back when I was young, my mom became a role model for me. She's confident, determined, motivated, friendly, happy and caring- a perfect blend. She jumped in when she was well out of her comfort level and opened her life to a world of experiences and people.

I knew since the age of eight, when I got to go to "bring your child to work day" at IBM, that I wanted to work for a big company (like my dad) and have a nice car. I wanted all the securities that came with a big company: 401k, salary, and benefits. I wanted to dress nicely, work nine to five and have weekends off. What could be better? In tenth grade all students were required to take a test aimed at figuring out what job we would be best suited for. My results? Data entry. I'm good with numbers and I'm shy and don't like to speak in groups. It wasn't exactly what I was looking for but I decided to work with it.

I FOLLOWED THE MASSES... FOR A DAY

When I graduated from college I spent the summer having fun and then it was time to get to work. My dream of working for a big company with a high salary and dressing up for work resurfaced. My dad set up an interview at IBM. The next day I was offered an entry-level job with an annual twenty-five thousand dollar salary, two weeks of vacation and full benefits. I was going to buy a BMW325i and be on my way. I went to bed that night thinking this was everything I had always wanted.

I could barely sleep that night. My inner wisdom was on high alert. Working at IBM wasn't truly what I wanted. I just got caught up in what I knew and the preset plan society sets-graduate college, get a nine-to-five job, work forty hours a week (and have no time for fun). I hadn't finished doing all I wanted to do before I "settled down". I needed to get some things out of my system, otherwise I would always wonder "what if?".

When I woke up in the morning, I told my dad I was turning down the job. He was incredibly disappointed but gave me my space, and also allowed me to have my first lesson in listening to myself and not making decisions based on what other people deem best. It's your life, and it's up to **you** to create the lifestyle that matches, he taught me.

WHAT DO YOU DO?

This is a question I love, one that always makes me pause and smile. Most people, when asked what they do, will answer what they do for a living, and even define themselves by this. "I'm a rocket scientist," "I'm a florist," or "I'm a yacht captain for high-end clientele." They may even go so far as to define themselves by what they used to do. "I'm an ex-corporate banker turned baker." It is certainly understandable, as most people spend so much time at work that they only do what they do for a living and don't do much else.

But you know as much as I that we are more than what we do for a living. How about "I invented the microchip that goes into outer space and love fiddling with homemade robots," "I love flowers and making arrangements that cheer people and am researching how flower essences increase people's healing," or "I make a kick-ass German chocolate cake, can free-dive fifty feet and play the ukulele every morning for an hour upon waking."

My hope is that after reading this book you will be able to answer this question with a full page of answers. Start defining yourself by how much fun you have and the things that make you feel truly alive. Start changing your mindset NOW from making a living to making a life.

This simple step of broadening your view on what you "do" is a great way to begin.

DO THIS: What Do You Do?

Answer the question of "What do you do?" by focusing on the things that excite and inspire you. "I compete in paddleboard contests around the world, write books about my adventures in life and business, and surf whenever possible."

Follow that with your talents and skills that you are proud of. "I'm a ballsy businesswoman who believes in my dreams and in the people who help make them happen." Finally, list any other things that you "do" that don't typically make it into conversations but you are just dying to share with people. "I make terrific quiche and sing falsetto in the shower."

THINK OUTSIDE THE BOX

So often we get stuck in our old routines because we can't see a way out of them. Sometimes what we want to do seems too far out of reach. Or worse, we don't even know what our dreams are anymore and we have no idea what inspires us. Maybe you have been doing the same thing for so long you don't know anything else, or maybe you are caught up in the swirl of someone else's dream and are lost, not knowing what direction to choose.

There are a few ways to make things happen, and it requires a little creativity on your part. But above all, **you** have to make things happen.

Don't settle for what's presented to you unless you are thrilled with the prospects. If you wait for things to present themselves on a platter you will go hungry. Making things happen will result in you creating your life the way **you** want it and will give you a sense of control that, when lacking, usually results in worry.

In short, if you want to change, seriously change, then you have to **do something different.**

Let's use the example of travel. Maybe you want to see the world but don't have the time or money. My first suggestion would be to listen to other people's experiences. You can truly travel through others, expand your life by listening to their

25

stories. You know your own life, your own stories. Stop talking and listen.

Then read travel magazines and books. Cut out pictures of places you want to travel to and put them on your dream board (more on that in a moment). If you have a home or apartment try house-swapping, where you live in someone's house and they live in yours for a certain agreed upon length of time. That alone takes care of your accommodation, usually your biggest expense. If you don't have a house to swap, you could try housesitting. Google it. See what options show up.

If you get your two week vacation and you do end up traveling, then renting a vacation house by owner is sometimes less expensive than a hotel. Live in the place you are visiting. You will meet locals and have more truly authentic experiences if you live in town rather than in a hotel with other tourists. Go with the flow and energy of a place rather than sticking to an itinerary.

If you really want to travel and don't have the time and can't afford it, there's always the option of becoming an airline attendant, working on a cruise ship or becoming a travel writer. Let someone pay **you** to see the world. It doesn't have to be your lifelong job but it opens up the world for you to travel.

How about college? It's expensive and many people don't go because they can't afford it. Enlist! The military will put you through college for free in exchange for duty. It's better to enlist and get a college education than to not go to college because you can't afford it. One of my friends enlisted in the Navy, went to dental technician school, lived on the base and it was all paid for by the Navy. She is now out of the Navy and works at a dental office.

There are always ways to make things happen. So research and create opportunities. They don't have to currently exist; the

26

more you research the more you can create ways.

Remember, there are only speed bumps, not roadblocks.

DO THIS: The Dream Board

One day, while staring at my computer my screen saver started running though all the pictures in My Pictures folder. I sat back and watched and realized how blessed I was to have great friends, travel, fun times dressing up and being goofy and so much more. I sat there and made two pages of pictures, with at least 20 pictures on each page. I went to the store and bought a poster board and mounted my pictures of the last year of my life on the board and hung it next to my closet where I could see it every day, multiple times a day.

I still spend a few minutes looking at it every night as part of my gratitude practice. The images have become ingrained in my subconscious, which help me think and feel this life everyday. I can't be sad when I look at these pictures.

I decided to use my "year in pictures board" as the center of my dream board. I also added things I want, places I want to visit, and things I am grateful for. It's a packed board, especially since I had to add a third page of pictures.

If you want a change, then start with the board. It's simple and fun and gets you thinking about what it is you really want. Add a place you would like to travel to, a pet you might want, a picture of yourself when you were fit that you would like to be like again. To get you started you need to find out what you like and desire. As these things enter your life you can take the picture down and add something else. Always keep it current with what you want.

If you don't have access to pictures, you could start gathering old magazines that interest you, or even ones others are willing to recycle your way (You just never know where you'll find inspiration!). Allow yourself the luxury to casually browse through them, tearing or cutting out any words or images that inspire or interest you. Soon enough you'll have a big pile to help you unveil what it is you long for.

Next, on your poster or foam core board, glue down the images and words in any arrangement that pleases you. Finish when you feel finished. Stand back and marvel at your dreams made real. Even though they are only on paper (for now), you will begin to consciously recognize what it is that motivates you.

Put your dream board in a prominent place and gaze upon it often. Watch how your world begins to shape itself based upon the images you gravitate towards.

LIMITATIONS AND RESTRICTIONS: THE EVIL "SHOULD"

We all want freedom to be who we are, to do what we want and love who we want. Many people complain about our government, believing it is at fault for taking away our freedom to do, speak and be, but the biggest culprit is usually ourselves, nudged along by overall society. So many of us tend to live our lives following the masses, restricting ourselves and limiting our creativity. Most people don't want to be the odd one out and stray, instead doing what they think they are supposed to.

In order for you to create the life you want, you will need to be brave. You need to trust that you can create your own path regardless of the fine opinions or approval of others. You don't have to know where your path is going to lead, or how you are going to get there. Just make sure you keep moving.

Any movement forward is a positive movement and growth towards your true you and a life that will make you feel like a millionaire.

If you lack motivation, I have a suggestion: starting with Googling video clips of Pat Croce in action or go to www.PatCroce.com. Pat is one of the most inspiring people I have met in my life as well as an amazing motivational speaker, business owner and friend. My favorite of Pat's speeches is about the word "should."

Pat says, "Have you ever found yourself saying 'I should work out more' or 'I should write that down,' or 'I should have bought that stock?" He then goes on to say you should "kick the "should" out of you." Stop saying the word "should." It implies lack of choice and lack of power. It's your life, you do as you see fit. Choose to do something, or choose not to. No "shoulds". Take the word "should" and cross it off your list.

Here's the cool thing about the word "should": It will help you understand what you do and do not like and act as a trigger to investigate why you feel blocked about certain things. If you find yourself saying "I should really do A, B, or C," you will probably see that underneath it all, "should" is linked to not really wanting to. Why? Only you can answer that. Check it out. It will help you understand yourself better.

Most of my life I have endlessly tread in unfamiliar territory creating my own path. I do it confidently because I know what I like and what I don't like. This allows me to powerfully lead from my heart, which knows nothing of should and only of what is true and real.

You don't have to know how to do something if you are calling the shots from your heart. The heart is powerful. Follow it, even if others don't.

DO THIS: List Your "Shoulds"

I should stop eating donuts. I should wake up earlier and exercise. I should drive a nicer car. I'm supposed to be making x amount of dollars at this age. I'm supposed to meet everyone out for drinks.

Now reread what you wrote. Which things feel true? Which feel powered by something outside of yourself? Which feel powered by your heart? What if you changed the word "should" and "supposed to" to "could?" Does it feel different? It gives YOU the power. You can choose. You can always choose.

DO THIS: Kick The Should Out of You

Just for a week, be conscious of when you use the word "should." Correct yourself aloud each time you do, replacing it with the word "could." Notice how often you say it, and how by choosing to replace it with the word "could" makes you feel. Did it give you back your sense of power? It's all your choice.

Another way we limit and restrict ourselves is with labels. People like to label things, put them in categories and give them a place. Labels comfort people. By saying, "I am a republican" instead of "I vote," or "I am a vegetarian" instead of "I eat what feels healthy to me" you categorize yourself, limiting your potential for change and growth. Why would you want to limit your life for yourself and for others to see?

Life is constantly changing and you want to feel free to change your views, your mind, and your actions. It is more than okay

30

to change your mind. It is critical. If you never change, you will never grow.

Poetry is a new thing for me, I'm not good at it but I do it. One of my earliest poems was on labels:

Labels
You are open
Accepting of all
Everything
This is new for you
Your reigns always so tight
You loosen them
But don't let go
Feelings you've never had before
Afraid to feel
Unafraid to think
Thinking creates restrictions
Feelings create openness
Acceptance
Trying to make sense
You make labels
Labels scare you
Your reigns are tightening
You need to let go
I want you to let go

Keep open. Don't fall into the comfort of categorizing and labeling. **Be open**.

THE PLAN OR "GUIDELINE"

Life rarely goes according to plan. If you ask anyone older than you about their plan they will likely tell you they had a plan and life didn't stick to it. They will probably even tell you they

31

would never have expected to be where they are now or that life did not go according to their plan but everything worked out in the end. So though it's good to have a plan to help give you some direction, also know it's ok to let it go, change it or rewrite it. Don't get hung up on "the plan."

When we are young, we have plans and dreams and then when we get older, we get deterred and often times really stuck in the patterns of the masses. I encourage you to break out of the norm. Find what it is you want to do and do it.

I will tell you right now that you will be the minority and may even feel like you are not on the right path. But it is those who break from the norm that feel fulfilled. If it was easy and normal then we would all be successful.

Breaking out of the norm will require a lot of "go-getum-ness." You might be up against naysayers, minimal support and the envy of many. You will succeed and you will fail as you make this break. Take it for what it is and keep moving. Don't get discouraged. You will find that life opens up to a whole world of new experiences and opportunities when you just keep breaking through and staying open to life's experiences.

And don't worry if it seems like your plan keeps changing. There is growth in change.

**DO THIS:** The Plan

Think back to "the plan" you may have had for your life. Does your current life match it? How do you feel about that? Do you have any new "plans" that swim through your head these days? Write them down. Look at them in a month. See if they still make sense. Laugh if they don't

CHAPTER THREE

EMBRACE CHANGE

*Insanity: doing the same thing
over and over again and
expecting different results.*
-*Albert Einstein*

Change is a fact of living, so embrace it! So many people are afraid of making change, of quitting their jobs, of moving to a new city. Most people are afraid of change because they are afraid of failure. But failure of what? What would really happen if you "failed?" What really is the worse case scenario? You can always go back if you have to. Change brings on new experiences and relationships.

I remember when I told everyone at the corporate company I was so "successful" with that I was moving to an island. One woman said something that I hear on a daily basis at the "job" I have now: "I wish I could do that." My response back then was that she could. She said, "But I have a job here and my car, my husband." My answer to that then and now is that there will always be excuses for not doing everything you want to do. If you really want to do something, you can, you will, and you must.

You can change your life.

There are two kinds of people- those that let life happen and those who take life by the horns. You have the power to make things happen. And remember, it is all right to change your mind. What holds people back is the idea that if something doesn't work out, they will have "failed," when maybe it just wasn't meant to. It's really a matter of perspective, so try shifting your feeling about the failure to a place of clarity. Know you tried and that "the plan" just didn't hold up.

If you open your mind and get yourself out of the failure feeling, you can usually see that another door has just opened. The more you can get into life and the experiences it offers, the more opportunities will arise. Opportunities will open up and you will have to decide which to choose.

PASS THE EARPLUGS, PLEASE

When you find the motivation and decide to make a positive change and move towards it, there will inevitably be people who try to stop you. It's human nature. People are comforted by consistency as they like knowing how it will all play out.

But do you stay in your job because your colleague or friend wants you to? Do you not lose weight because your partner doesn't? If you want to lose weight then get up early, go for a walk, eat smaller portions. If your partner then tries to convince you otherwise, that person is not supporting you in what you want. You might want to take a closer look at your relationship. It's hard enough to get to the realization that you need to make a change but to have someone tell you "you can't do it" makes it even harder.

A lot of the time it is those who are closest to you who try to keep you down. This is why most people don't change. They don't want to upset anyone. Maybe they feel they are being selfish. I've got news for you: ultimately, you've got to look out for numero uno, your self. If you don't care about yourself, then no one else will.

Stay focused and realize that maybe they are just jealous or fearful, or something that is a far cry from supportive. Lead the way to change. Do what you want and realize you may lose some people along the way.

When I was in high school I hung out with most of the people from the class younger than me. I was insecure and wanted people to like me but I wasn't smart or funny and I was also shy. But I was great at sports, so good that I thought I could casually get through practice and still compete with the best. I wanted to be liked and I was because I had one great talent...I could buy beer from a liquor store with my fake ID. This meant I was always invited to parties. I started to drink all the time, becoming reckless and heading down a bad path.

My father saw this and decided to offer me a challenge- to run a marathon, 26.2 miles. He wanted me to train for fifteen weeks with him and as long as I ran the mileage on the training program he laid out, he would take me to London to see my family. The challenge came across with an underlying sense that I couldn't do it. As a cocky high school kid I thought I could do anything, so of course I took the challenge. I figured I could train **and** party. I was in high school after all.

The training program started with running two to three miles a day, five days a week. This was easy in the beginning, but as the mileage increased weekly, I had to get up earlier and earlier before school to run. Interestingly, the more fit I felt the less I wanted to drink. I stopped going to parties and joined the track team so I could do extra miles after school.

Of course my "friends" didn't support me in my training. In fact, they were mad that I wasn't going to parties since I was the one who supplied the beer. It was hard going from one of the cool kids to having no friends at all. I was heartbroken.

BE WHO YOU WANT TO BE AND YOU WILL EVENTUALLY BE SUPPORTED

Over time, I started to hang out after practice with my new track friends. They actually liked me for who I really was (as much as you know who you really are in high school). Near the end of my fifteen weeks of training I was running 53 miles in my five days of training a week. My track friends would run all the extra miles with me after our regular track practice, supporting me in my personal challenge. True friends to be sure.

I traveled to London with my dad and together we ran the London Marathon in a run time of three hours and forty-nine minutes. It was one of the best days of my life. I cried. In the fifteen weeks of training I had lost so much of what I thought was important and in turn found out what really was.

To this day, those fifteen weeks of training are the single biggest factor in who I have become today. I'm glad my dad put forth the challenge because if he had just told me to stop drinking I probably would have drank more. It was the single biggest positive change I made in my life. I definitely wouldn't be where I am today had I not changed my ways and found what was right for me. Thank you Dad!

Whether they believe you can do it or not, a true friend will support you. It is especially hard when you have a "friend" saying "you can't do it." If you believe them you will fail. Move past it, keep focused and use their disbelief in you to light a fire.

Often times, in the beginning, it seems that the more changes you make, the more people will try to hold you back. They want to keep you at their level, or worse, maybe even beneath them so they can feel more powerful. As you keep making changes, you will find yourself surrounded by people who care about you and support you. **These** are the people to rally by your side and listen to.

Stay motivated, keep true to what it is you want to do or find the change and be sure you are doing it for yourself. Hopefully your success will motivate the key players in your life and, at best, you will all grow together.

DO THIS: Who Are Your Allies?

While it's important to note the folks who aren't on your side, it's even more so to remember the ones who are. Think of the people in your life who, through thick and thin, you know you can count on; your dear old dad, who encouraged you to run a marathon, your amazing friend Elisa, who introduced you to the power of dreams and always brings you treats when you're down, your doctor, who supported you through your back pain and rallied you to find healing within instead of going under the knife.

Maybe there is someone from your past you can remember; your Aunt Bess, who always came with homemade chicken soup when you were sick, the art teacher who told you how talented you were, the neighbor who always bought the candy bars and candles you had to sell for French Club. Write down their names and numbers. Call or send them a card, thanking them for the encouragement so long ago.

MY STORY

When I resigned from my corporate job they asked me to stay, hoping I may change my mind. However, I was moving to Key West. So they asked me to continue to travel to work accounts from Key West. I decided to help them out but that meant I was living in paradise but always flying somewhere else around the country. I simply didn't want to leave the island.

Six months later, I got a call telling me they were terminating my job. My boss, the nice one, sensed my surprise and questioned my response. Even though I knew deep down that it was coming, I still felt rejected and a little hurt. Also, there was a sense of security that came with salary and benefits.

I drove home a little teary-eyed, got my journal that I never wrote in and went to the back dock by the water and got all my feelings out on paper. Then I called my sister. She said, "That's great! You have wanted more time in Key West and you have all these ideas. Now you have time to do them."

Wow, she was right! In an instant my despair was replaced with excitement and opportunity. I couldn't wait to see what the next phase of my life had in store for me.

IT'S OK IF YOU DON'T KNOW WHAT YOU WANT TO DO

I began writing down a list of all the things I wanted to do, including some business ideas, swimming with dolphins, buying a boat and getting a dog. I could be an internet stock day trader, set up a business as an errand girl, or open a retail store. While I explored my ideas and options, I spent every day kayaking.

One new phase of my life included my spirituality. At the time I had none and didn't know much about it. I was searching for something. I would bring spiritual books out in my kayak and float around in shallow clear water with the sunny, eighty-degree weather and read. I really didn't know what I wanted specifically. I just knew I wanted to run my own business.

One day I was sitting outside on the dock reading and I saw a bunch of kayakers paddle over to a marina. "That looks fun," I thought. Maybe I would lead kayak tours. I never thought about *how* I would lead a tour or that I knew nothing about Key West and the waters. I just thought it looked fun.

Later I went for a bike ride to scope out the kayak company located on Stock Island, a run-down area just over the bridge from where I lived, at a marina at the end of the road. Across the water I could see the roof of the house I was renting. I saw kayaks and an employee. I asked him if they were hiring. He directed me to a guy getting in a flats fishing boat.

I went up to the man, never getting off my bike and introduced myself. His name was Jonathan and he ran the kayak company with his friend Greg. I asked if he was hiring. He replied casually, "If you want to work and you promise me I never have to get in another kayak again then, you're hired." All he wanted to do was fish. He hired me on the spot for $6.75 an hour. It was a bit of a pay cut from my corporate salary, but it wasn't the money I was focused on. I was now going to be doing something fun.

When I lived in Connecticut, I always stressed about money. My job security was in someone else's hands, a company that made random Christmas week clean-outs of employees. Sometimes it would be a top-producing salesman, sometimes it was the last on the totem pole. There was no value for employee dedication. When I moved to Key West, I actually got myself out of credit card debt and created my first savings account. Materialistic things were just not important any longer. Now, I was on the water every day, commuting one hundred yards by kayak over the channel separating Key West from Stock Island.

I was so excited to be working. I had no idea what I was doing and that made it all the more fun. The training was basic at best. The guys took me out on the water, showed me the kayak tour route and then left me on my own. The next day I lead my first tour. When I returned from a trip I never knew if I had another trip. If people were waiting I would go out again. If not, I just locked everything up and went home. I was living in the moment and soaking it all in.

The only other employee in the company was Dennis, the

39

driver. I only saw him when he arrived with the fifteen passenger van full of people off the cruise ship and when he met us after. I was reliable and Dennis was professional and precise: we made a good team. The guys we were working for weren't ever really around. Since they didn't seem to care much about the business, we were pretty much running the show.

One day when I showed up to work, Jonathan was there. I was surprised to see him and even more surprised when he told me he had to fire me. He found a girl from the JC Penny store willing to work for six dollars an hour, seventy five cents less an hour than me. I was shocked, but shook his hand and got on my bike making a point not to burn any bridges. I rode home dumbfounded, but with a strong feeling this wouldn't be the end.

When I worked corporate and they would have their mass firings, I would worry that I would be next. I had a conversation about it with my work friend Ron who was older and one of the company's best salesmen. His simple response, "If they fire you, you just find another job." Ron had this overwhelming belief that because he was a great employee, he had no doubt that he would find another job.

I'd always wanted to feel that kind of security, to relieve my worry and have that much faith in myself. I never had faith until on that particular day when I was actually let go. Ron was right.

DO WHAT YOU LOVE AND THINGS WILL FALL INTO PLACE

I occupied my time kayaking with another company, Mosquito Coast, but just as a tag-along customer. They did wonderful, four-hour kayak and snorkel trips. I would bring a pen (my NASA space pen that can write on oil or water) and paper and go kayaking with this company every day. I felt like I was in a floating school.

When I wasn't kayaking I would work in the boatyard helping boat owners fix up their boats. I knew nothing about boats but I figured it would be a great way to learn. No one ever wants to work in the boatyard, so I thought it would be easy to get work. I still had no idea what I wanted to do but I was learning and growing, which was exactly what I felt I ought to be doing since I didn't know what else to do.

About two weeks later the Mosquito Coast Kayaks offered me a job. I took it. This time I was offered ten dollars an hour to be on my own with a handful of customers. This particular trip always intimidated me because it was an in-depth eco tour that had a very intelligent, nature-observing customer base. The clients expected knowledge and expertise.

Though I spent every free moment reading and learning about the near-shore waters of the Florida Keys, I was also dealing with the issue of my shyness. If you get me in front of more than three people I am mush. I was so nervous. I don't think I ever got over my nerves, which were on constant overload.

I am still not sure why I put myself in that position aside from the fact that I'm always up for a challenge. There really is no other way to grow.

DO THIS: Unlimited Resources: Imagine It!

What would you do if time wasn't an issue and you didn't have to worry about money, your age or your skill level? Make a list, similar to a bucket list of all the things big and small you would do with your time. Not the things you would buy, but the things you would do.

Let's take this even further now and say you were to intern at five different places, doing something that interested you. Would you work behind the scenes at ESPN, work at a law firm, in the front office of a major sports team, work for an architect, cook at a restaurant, design websites for Disney, teach at a school?

This is a good start to figuring out what you want to do and where you want to spend your time. You can then work backwards and figure out how to get there.

We usually fill our free time with "the usual" and things we know instead of the new things we want to try.

BELIEVE IN YOUR VALUE SO OTHERS WILL TOO

About the same time I got this job, Dennis called me to say one of the owners of the company was coming into town and wanted to talk to me. I thought Jonathan was the owner. It turned out he was just the manager for a couple of guys who live in Canada. I wasn't sure what the meeting was about but I met with Steve, a nice man, who was a half owner of the company along with another Canadian man named David. Steve flew all the way to Key West to ask me if I'd be interested in running his company at $1,500 a month. He was dissatisfied with Jonathan and Gregory and said I came highly recommended by Dennis.

Was I interested? Hell yes! But not at $1,500 a month. He then offered $1,800. Though this was a lot more than my original $6.75 an hour, I knew my value and still couldn't accept the opportunity. There began the negotiations of a bonus package, in which my value was included in the offer. I accepted the $1,800 monthly base and a bonus of one dollar for every cruise ship passenger and two dollars for every non-ship customer.

At the time the business consisted only of cruise ship contracts where people would pre-book a kayak excursion in Key West and Dennis would pick them up at the dock. It was just under a $50,000 a year company. Steve asked me to restructure the company. He kept the line of communication open, and said to call if I needed anything. Of course Jonathan was very displeased, telling me I'd never be able to handle it. Little did he know that those words only gave me more fuel to succeed.

To make things easier, I set everything in my name as the owners lived in Canada. I worked the company like it was my own. In fact, everyone in town thought it was mine. I would answer the phone, take reservations, pick people up in the van, take them on a tour and drive them back. Because I was considered the new company in town, it was an uphill battle. But I saw the money potential in my bonus rather than my salary so when customers would try to give me a tip after the tour I would not accept it and instead I would ask them to go back to their hotel concierge or ship excursions desk and tell them that they had a great time. Business skyrocketed. The company grew three times its gross in two years.

During the next two years I had to make a few changes. One was letting my position go at Mosquito Coast, which I was so very sad about. I told them I was leaving but I had a replacement, my girlfriend Robyn. She loved that job.

I made another change, I had to hire people, not only because the business was growing, but I had just broken my leg running and jumping over a puddle. On the way home from the hospital we stopped by Blockbuster to rent a movie. That's were I ran into my friend Michelle. Yes, I hired my first employee, a friend, in the Action/Drama section of Blockbuster.

SOMETIMES YOU HAVE TO STEP ASIDE IN ORDER TO GROW

One of the hardest things to do in a business run by one person is to hire another. When it's just you, you are in charge of the outcome. When someone else is working for you, you have to trust they will do a good job and suffer the consequences when they don't.

In this case, I had to hire someone else. It was that or lose customers. With my leg in an air cast wrapped in a plastic bag, I trained Michelle. I threw Michelle into the mix much like I had been when I had been hired. She ended up being great. Because of her addition to the company we grew. Without having another person to help we would have stunted our growth. I was able to get off the water some days and focus on other aspects of the business that needed attending to.

Sometimes we push and push and push the limits of what we can do. What we don't realize is that we would get a lot farther if we just stepped aside.

Outdoor Adventure was taking off and out of the blue the owner of Mosquito Coast told me he was retiring and offered me his business. He insisted that Robyn and I take it over. I didn't have much money saved but he made it affordable. Thanks to good credit from my old job, I was approved for a bank loan. The irony was I was operating a company I didn't own and I owned a company I didn't operate. So I got more involved. During the next five years I ran both companies and had the time of my life.

But then I got antsy. The businesses had become too easy to run. There are plenty of people who like what they do, have their routine and don't like change, but that's not for me. I need to grow. I thought it was time to focus on the business I owned and build and grow my own company rather than someone else's company. One of the owners of Outdoor Adventure, David, came down to meet with me and before I had a chance to give my resignation, he offered me his half of the business. I was excited... until he told me he wanted $140,000. "Wait a minute," I thought to myself. "You want $140,000 for half of a company that I built for you? No thanks!!!!!!!!"

He eventually got down to $120,000 and I was sick to my stomach. I did not see this coming. He wanted cash and I didn't have that kind of money. He told me if I didn't take it he would put up his half for sale in a kayak magazine. Ouch! He was a shrewd businessman, never recognizing or showing gratitude for building his $50,000 company into a $300,000 company in two years.

I was so hurt by his offer, it reminded me of the corporate world where business is business and it doesn't matter if you showed up early and left late, missed family events and dinners, forfeited all your vacation time and dedicated yourself to your job.

LAZY DOG ADVENTURES IS BORN

What David didn't understand was the value of **me** in the business he was selling. The town thought it was my company because I was the face of it. Everything was in my name and credit, from the phone bill to the lease to additional cruise ship contracts. David expressed to me that if I wasn't interested he would sell his half to anyone he could find. My options were to pay him $120,000 for a company that I helped grow or be a shrewd business woman and start up my own business for $10,000 in kayaks and brochures and have a turn-key business with my reputation firmly established. The lease was in my name.

I called my best friend Dave and told him the situation.

Adventurers together, we had wanted to go into business with each other for years. We did everything with our border collies Camillo and Molly by our sides. We had gone as far as selling Dave's new Lazy Dog design tee shirt to my kayak customers. I had the customer base and he had the shirts. There was a divine chemistry of the kayak and tee shirts.

In fact, that very day, the business leasing the marina store next to my kayak shack had a lease fall through. It was perfect timing. There was our shop, much bigger than expected, falling into our laps.

Though it would have been way cheaper to buy our own kayaks and print up brochures, we had to stay true to our integrity. It didn't feel right to shut down David, who had given me the opportunity to begin with. So bestie Dave and I took out money from our houses and got a bank loan for the rest and paid David the $120,000 cash. Two years later we decided to buy Steve out of his half of Outdoor Adventure. It was a lot of money to come up with, but with the help of investors (mostly friends and family), we raised it and the business was entirely ours.

So what started out as floating around in the waters in a kayak while reading some good books helped me dare to dream became Lazy Dog Adventures, the business I run today.

As you can see, there were some twists and turns along the way and it wasn't exactly your ordinary business derived from a solid business plan. But by tuning in to what felt authentic to me and saying "no" to what didn't, listening to my instincts, being willing to stay open and aligning myself with the right people at the right time, my life as a Millionaire in Flip Flops slowly took shape.

Put simply, I found my passion and made it my life's work. And you can, too.

CHAPTER FOUR

WHERE DO YOU START?

If today were the last day of my life, would I want to do what I am about to do today? And whenever the answer has been "no" for too many days in a row, I know I need to change something.
-Steve Jobs

What if you don't know what you want to do? Then try **everything!** Plain and simple. As you begin, to try pay attention to what you like in people, places and things--and pay attention to what you don't like, too. Knowing what you don't like helps you set your boundaries and keep your energy fields clear.

Once you've established what you **do** like, don't just settle in that comfort zone. Consider what you might like but haven't yet experienced. Push yourself to new things. Doing something new opens up your senses. Think of the first time you did something and how energizing and exciting it was. The unknown puts your senses on overload. The more you do the same thing, the more your senses dull and you switch to autopilot. For most this brings comfort. But remember, we are not looking for comfort--we are looking for energy, excitement and newness. So shake it up.

When my parents retired, they decided to take a continuing education college course. They were sixty, and in all of their sixty years, were never musically inclined. My dad enrolled in guitar lessons and my mom took singing lessons. My dad is now in a band, and my mom sang *Latin* in a recital and now they travel together to convalescent homes with my dad's band and perform. (They never could have planned this!).

I am going to constantly remind you of this throughout the

book. The more you do, the more alive you will feel. Take a look at your life and ask yourself: "Am I trying to live or am I just trying to stay alive?"

Justin Timberlake was once asked in an interview what his priority was: music, or movies? He responded by saying that his priority is inspiration. Why not do everything there is to do if you have the opportunity?"

One of my employees is from the Czech Republic. He came to the States, fell in love and got married. Sounds fairly ordinary, but I assure you, this guy is beyond ordinary. In fact, he constantly amazes me with all he does. Besides working for me he operates his own landscaping business. His thirst for knowledge is unquenched. Since moving here he has learned how to ride a motorcycle and then bought one. Then he auditioned for and got a part in a play. He rented space at a studio and taught Capoeira classes. Currently he is taking college classes in marine biology. He learned photography, got certified in SCUBA diving, made mini movies and travels the world with a backpack... and it goes on and on.

I asked him one day what drives him. He explained that opportunities in the Czech Republic are limited, so here he wanted to do it all. I was struck by his motivation, the drive with which he was living life. So many Americans have all this opportunity at their fingertips and they take it for granted. It was eye opening.

Constantly learn and you will constantly grow. Your mind will stay young and vibrant. Even if you're not good at it, trying new things will allow you to either check it off of your list and move on or open up a completely different door you never knew was there in the first place.

DO THIS: Out With The Old, In With The New

Below is a list of some simple ideas to begin your new life of living. They will help spark your desire to live life. Newness stimulates your mind and gets your heart racing, so the more "new" you can bring into your life the more you will begin living.

Take a different route to work or run a different path.
If you work out at the same time each day pick a different time.
If you get up and go to sleep at the same time then get up earlier or go to sleep later.
Try new restaurants or bars.
Shop at a different grocery store.
Learn a new skill, such as throwing pottery or guitar.
Take a college class.
Ask people to join you in all you do.
Ask lots of questions, and really listen.
Buy and try new and different foods.
Read magazines that seem interesting to you.
Just do it all.

 DO THIS: Get To Know Yourself

Make a list of all your roles. Are you a mom, a sister, a teacher? Then take all your roles and put them in a safe place. The roles you play are an important part of who you are.

Now as you are stripped from your roles and stand there naked, how do you feel? Are you sad, anxious, poor, worried, tired?

By understanding what your underlying feelings, emotions and needs are you can then begin to work on what it is you need. If you're tired, you need rest. If you're angry, you need forgiveness. When we are aware of our raw self we can begin to see what we need and fix what ails us.

49

ACTION PLANS

Action plans can help you set goals and call them into being by doing, instead of thinking or daydreaming. That is why they call it an "action" plan, after all.

In the book <u>What They Don't Teach You in the Harvard Business School,</u> Mark McCormack recounts a study conducted on students in the 1979 Harvard MBA program. In that year, the students were asked, "Have you set clear, written goals for your future and made plans to accomplish them?" Only three percent of the graduates had written goals and plans; thirteen percent had goals, but they were not in writing; and a whopping 84 percent had no specific goals at all.

Ten years later, the members of the class were interviewed again, and the findings, while somewhat predictable, were nonetheless astonishing. The 13 percent of the class who had goals were earning, on average, twice as much as the 84 percent who had no goals at all. And what about the three percent who had clear, written goals? They were earning, on average, ten times as much as the other 97 percent put together.

DO THIS: Ready? Set? Action!

Get out a pen and write down your ultimate wish list. Think big. Don't limit yourself with your realistic mind. Don't use the word "no." Don't think something is impossible. Write down your goals for the following: Job. Relationship. Finances. Health. Spirituality. Creativity. But don't stop there. Go towards what you truly would like your life to be like.

Once you have done this with NO LIMITS, you will then

figure out how you are going to do it with the help of your "Action Plan," which we'll get to in a moment.

And just so you know, this is just an exercise to get your mind on board with what your heart wants. You don't actually have to know how this is all going to work, you just have to believe it. If your total self gets on board, the better the chances it will happen. The next section will help you figure out how.

So, what do you want out of life? Right here, right now? I want you to make a list of what you want your life to be like, a year from now and five years from now. Put as much information down as you possibly can.

This will be one of your most valuable tools for becoming your very own version of a Millionaire in Flip Flops. Your action plan can include ideas around your work, your finances, your lifestyle, your health. For example:

- What do you want to do for work?
- What will do with your free time?
- What hobbies do you have or would like to have?
- Where do you want to travel and with whom?
- What would you like your relationships to be like?
- What do you want your finances to be like?
- What would you like the details of your typical day to look like?
- What things have you always wanted to do but haven't?

DO THIS: Short and Long Term Goals

Now work with the list above and make a plan. What are your

goals? Where do you want to be financially, in your relationships, your work life, physically--in a year, five years, ten years? This is important work for you. If you have no solid thoughts here then life will happen to you. By creating this plan for yourself you will make life happen for you.

Don't just think about it; write it all down. The best part is that you don't have to know how it will all work out. The challenge is in learning to believe that it will.

Make sure these are the goals that you set for yourself--not your parents' or your spouse's goals for you. There's no power in those goals. Be sure to think about it. Write it down, clearly and with as much detail as you can, then read it every day. Your chances for making your dream life come true are better if you read it regularly, so don't just write your list and forget about it.

When reading through this book, keep this list handy. Pin it somewhere where you can see it. Keep referring to it. Most of the action plans that are in this book will work on changing your lifestyle to the one you want. Use this list as your lifestyle goal and feel free to add to it as you go. You want to see this list change into the lifestyle you want.

What might feel like small or even insignificant adjustments will ultimately adjust the course of your destination. And the more adjustments you make, the more progress you will make. Any step is movement. This is not a quick fix to your life but rather a plan involving small changes to how you do things--and more importantly--how you think about things that will create the life you desire.

Hopefully you have already put the book down and made your list. If you didn't, do it now. After you do, read it. Daily.

THE TIME IS NOW

Don't wait until you finish this book. Don't wait until Monday. Action starts now! It doesn't have to be a life changing action but it does have to be something, no matter how small, that you want to change. Today you will make a forward movement, and move forward, even if it's only an inch.

Action is not about thinking, it's about doing. Thinking you will eat healthier is not making you healthier. Thinking you will volunteer is not helping anyone. DO your thoughts. What can you do today to start? Do you want to get fit? Then join a gym, buy some weights or a workout CD. Make some action NOW! Get yourself moving.

FAILURE IS IN NOT DOING

If you are out there really going for it, there is no such thing as failure--only experiences to learn from. So maybe things didn't pan out the way you thought or hoped. Experiences well-reflected upon lead to growth. If thinking of failure as experiences seems too far of a stretch, you can think of them as mistakes. Everyone makes mistakes. But what good is it to dwell on your mistakes? Don't let it get you down. Instead, take responsibility for your mistakes and move on.

About twelve years ago, just after I had met my new best friend and future business partner Dave we decided to do something I can now look back on and say, "Wow. That was stupid."

We decided to go to the Dry Tortugas, located seventy miles west of Key West. For those of you who don't know, the Dry Tortugas is the least visited National Park, primarily because it is so hard to get there. You can either take a two and a half hour ferry or a thirty minute seaplane ride. We decided to kayak! Dave, our friend Jim and I left from Key West at 8pm, just after a thunderstorm came through and soaked us. We would paddle through the night keeping us out of the sun. The trip would take about two days.

The first four hours were beautiful, paddling into the sunset. Then it got dark and we couldn't see a thing, including each other. We were paddling over fairly shallow waters, about six to ten feet of water and occasionally something would knock into our kayaks, presumably large fish. We all were a little uneasy but didn't say much, just paddled closer together.

We seemed to be getting off track. Jim was navigating by the stars and Dave had all the latest gear including a GPS. The current was so strong that we needed to take a break and regroup but there was nowhere to rest. Then the guys started disagreeing about which way to go. I felt uneasy so I just kept quiet. It turned out the reason I was uneasy was because I was sea sick, and I proceeded to throw up for the next three miles.

We came to land twenty-two miles from Key West, a place called the Marquesas--a beautiful group of islands created by a meteor. It was almost day break and we all needed a rest. We tied our kayaks together and floated in the middle of the Marquesas as the sun began to rise.

In case you wonder why we didn't actually get out and take a break here at the lovely Marquesas, I should clarify the word "islands" here. The Marquesas are actually clusters of mangroves: salt-tolerant trees with incredible root systems, very little accumulated land, and incredible amounts of mosquitoes and no-see-ums. You can hear the mosquitos from a half mile away. Not exactly a hospitable place to hang your hammock.

So, there we were along its shore. We were sweltering, our boats knocking each other and keeping us awake. The next leg of the trip would be forty-eight miles and would include Rebecca Channel, one of the strongest currents in the Keys, along with deep water and no islands in which to break. We stood off shore in four feet of water so we could stretch our bodies.

This was when I decided it wouldn't be a good idea for me to continue. I was dehydrated and exhausted from throwing up. Jim agreed and said we should head back to Key West. Dave said he would like to continue on. The boys argued and Jim paddled away, back to Key West. I didn't know what to do. I was relying on these two because I was new to these waters.

Dave used his radio, calling any boats in the area to see if they could assist. It was no easy task for them to locate us, but after two hours, a big yacht picked me up. It was a husband and wife who were selling their boat and taking it on one last trip to the Dry Tortugas. I got on board as Dave instructed me on his plan. Once I got to the Tortugas, I would jump on the ferry, which would leave at 3pm and get a ride back to Key West. Dave was going to continue on and follow his GPS, which was tracked to follow the same path as the ferry. He told me to tell the ferry captain to listen to his radio on the return in case he got in trouble.

Aboard the yacht, I passed out, awakening occasionally to a lady offering me water and pretzels and sitting by me to make sure I was all right. The boat was beautiful but slow. So slow that it looked like we wouldn't make it to the Dry Tortugas before the ferry left. As we approached land the ferry was leaving. The yacht captain radioed over to the ferry and they waited for me. I got on the ferry and sat in the back, deflated and embarrassed as a hundred passengers and a crew that I knew all looked at me.

I moved up front and asked the captain to listen to the radio. We searched for Dave on the trip home and listened closely for his voice. After about an hour of travel, we heard a signal. It was Dave, panicking. "Pick me up, pick me up," he shouted.

We searched and eventually found him, luckily on the same GPS track as the boat. Dave couldn't stand. He was dehydrated and needed help out of the kayak. We sat together on the back of the boat, silent, totally deflated. No one said anything to us, either. It might have been because we stunk like we hadn't showered in days.

We arrived back at the dock at 5:30 p.m. and realized Jim hadn't made it back. Friends went out in boats to look for him and found him floating in his kayak about a mile off shore. He was brought in, exhausted, sunburnt and had burned his eyes so badly (he had forgotten his sunglasses) that he ended up with permanent eye damage.

We didn't talk to each other for days. We were all disappointed and embarrassed. We were the talk of the town because everyone heard the radio calls for help and now everyone knew who the morons were that tried to kayak to the Dry Tortugas. Years later I would still hear people talk about the story and I would say, "That was me."

We didn't make that trip a success, however a few months later Dave completed the trip, paddling during the day and sleeping on three inches of bird crap at the top of a buoy tower in the middle of the ocean at night. I would not try again.

For many years it felt like a failure, but now I can view it as one of my crazy, memorable adventures that make me who I am. True failure exists when you don't try at all.

This is prevalent in ideas. Everyone has them but few act on them. Do you have ideas to explore? If so, make them happen. I can't tell you how many people have told me of their ideas-- and some of them are good--but they never do them. I'm guilty of this too.

Have you ever had an idea and then a year later someone makes a business out of your idea? Be the minority, take a risk, act on an idea, put yourself in the game and make it work. This is what sets you apart from everyone else.

I always thought that successful people were the ones who had ideas. It wasn't until I had my own business that I realized this is not the case. Successful people are the ones who can make it happen. Most ideas don't take a lot of money, they just take your time so manage your time properly and dedicate a certain amount of time to making your idea come to life.

If your idea is an invention and you don't know how to make it happen, pull from your resources: there are many. The Patent and Trademark website is full of information. Go to the library, read books, talk to friends. You can use a company that helps develop your ideas and in turn takes a percentage of the profits, or you can find a manufacturer on your own.

Don't take yourself out of the picture. Try with all you have and if it doesn't work out you can feel good about moving on. There is so much to do in this life and you don't want an "I should have (insert dream here)" to occupy any of your head or heart space. The main difference between successful people and unsuccessful people are successful people actually DO THINGS.

What are you afraid of? Failure? It's a failure if you don't act on your ideas. You will always wonder "What if?" You might not know where to start, but just do something--anything--to put your idea in motion. All it takes is a small step and that will lead to another step and momentum will build from there. What we fear doing most is usually what we most need to do. Remember, you don't want to be like most. So make yourself different and do something.

SAY YES TO EVERYTHING

A few years ago my fifteen year relationship ended and I found myself not knowing who I was as an individual and suddenly had extra time on my hands. I spent a few days depressed in the house until my friend Holly told me to watch a movie called "Yes Man." It's about a man who is unhappy in his life and decides to say "yes" to everything, even things he doesn't want to do. His life OPENS UP. He is exposed to new adventures, people and places.

I decided to follow in "Yes Man's" footsteps and my life turned into a crazy adventure for the next couple of years. Here's a summary of what happened, some of which are the most memorable times (good and bad) I've ever had, many of which were first-time experiences.

I began to travel, even though flying has been a fear of mine my entire life. I went to Hawaii, Mykonos, Madrid, Costa Rica, California, Puerto Rico, Bali then circumnavigated the world. I surfed in Kauai, hiked the Na-Pali Coast with a thirty-five pound pack, got high, did the Bikram Yoga challenge, went horseback riding, whitewater rafting, zip-lining and skydiving.

I won money paddle boarding, wrote my first poem, climbed a tree, and dressed up for costume parties as a roller derby girl, a lion fish, a pink flamingo in a pink tutu, a zombie, and a geisha girl, then organized my own inappropriate "pasties" party.

I hurt my back and was flat out for three weeks, where all nine doctors I went to told me I had to have back surgery. I lost two houses, lost twelve pounds and gained more new true friends than I can count. I moved four times, sometimes coming home to those new homes when the sun came up.

I won the East Coast Paddle board Championships and the co-ed softball team championship. I got arrested on my paddle board (though not charged) as I paddle boarded out to a friend of a friend's eight million dollar boat with my dog and drank wine, went to a strip club, fell off my bike and slept next to the toilet.

I cured my life long back pain thanks to a Chinese medicine doctor, chased waterspouts on my boat, almost got struck by lightning numerous times, caught a sailfish, and boated in the biggest, roughest waves I've ever boated in.

I paddle boarded around Key West, ended my fifteen-year relationship and sold almost all of my belongings, fell off my boat while I was driving it, fell in love, fell out of love.

And in the last few years, I laughed and cried more than any other time in my life. All because I made my favorite word "yes."

Although this list isn't all good things I will tell you I have **never felt more alive** than in the past few years and I will continue to say "yes." I don't focus on the tears or bruises to my body or ego for I know I am truly living to my potential.

Looking back at all the joy and challenges, I know that it's my choice in how I see these past few years. Was it the best or the worst? You know it--it was the best! My life has been full of the highest highs I've felt as well as the lowest of lows. I call that living. I know that the lows won't be around forever but I also know that the highs won't be around forever, either. So when I'm in it, I feel it, I embrace it, and then move on from it. I don't own it.

Life is constantly changing, I have no idea what's in store. With that in mind, I look forward to seeing how it all takes shape.

THE DESTINATION IS JUST THE EGO

59

All the things I listed above are really not what it's about but are what most people can relate to. "I went to Bali" or "I lost (or won) a paddleboard race." It's the ego. I get to tell people I did something and even if they haven't experienced it themselves they can understand it. But what these experiences are about for me really is the journey in them all. All the learning, tears, heartache, fear, bruises and joy that I experienced leading up to the end result.

The end result is useless, except for the ego. You finished a marathon, you wrote a book. There was a lot more self-awareness, growth and living in all that lead up to these destinations. It's all that leads up to the end where the transformation within you happens. How you deal with the daily training, the sacrifices, the adjustments as you worked to complete a goal--it's the process that matters most.

This is where growth happens. This is the stuff that makes it impossible for you to ever go back to your old life. This is living. So when you are going through it, live it, embrace it. It's what life is all about. The experiences. So just say "yes" and see what happens.

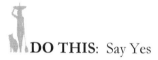

DO THIS: Say Yes

Be your own "Yes Man" for seven days straight and see what happens. Even if it makes you uncomfortable, say "yes" and see where it takes you. If someone asks you to go out, say "yes." If someone says would you like to try my meal, say "yes." If someone asks you to do them a favor, say "yes." If there isn't anyone to ask you to do something, then find something yourself.

Say yes to everything. At the end of the week, write down all the things you did. See how surprised you are.

CHAPTER FIVE

IT'S UP TO YOU

A life spent making mistakes is not only more honorable,
but more useful than a life spent doing nothing.
-George Bernard Shaw

Excuses are the number one nemesis to growth, goals, and generally anything surrounding success and happiness. If you want something bad enough you will find a way. So often we get in the way, saying things like "I can't," "I won't," and "I don't." They sound like reasons, but don't let them fool you. They are excuses in disguise. They flow all too easily and all too often.

Since successful people don't make excuses, while you have your eye on the prize as your own version of a Millionaire in Flip Flops, start wiping excuses right out of your vocabulary now!

News flash: we all have "things going on" or are "too busy" so don't ever use those phrases as excuses. It reeks of ego and no one wants to hear it. On the other end of the spectrum is your sense of confidence; we all have our "stuff" so don't devalue yourself by using excuses. There are no excuses and no one wants to hear them.

And if you are so bold as to tell someone that "I'm sorry I didn't come through for you but I have a lot going on right now," it minimizes what is going on in their life because they too "have a lot going on." The difference might be is that they showed up. Suck it up and make no excuses.

We all have "a lot going on." Pay attention to this and you will

61

realize how many excuses you make on a daily basis. Stop it!

DO THIS: What Your Excuses Are Worth: Not Much!

In the next three days, become completely aware, or as aware as you possibly can, of how often you find yourself making excuses.

This is no easy task, as often our excuses disguise themselves as our "reality." Tune in for words like: "I would but...", "I will tomorrow..." , "I am too tired...", "I don't know how...", "When I have more money/time/any suitable word here..." and the most blatant "I can't" and "It's just not possible."

Don't beat yourself up once you realize how often you participate in excuse-making. Just take notice of when you do it, and how it makes you FEEL. Probably not very powerful, or in charge of your life, right? Do you feel any closer as a Millionaire in Flip Flops or are your excuses limiting your reach?

Here's the catch: The best part of knowing that you make excuses (and most everyone does) is that you now know you have the power to *not* make an excuse. It's really your choice, though your conditioned behavior may have fooled you into thinking otherwise. With a little awareness and practice, this conditioned behavior of making an excuse can shift the other way.

With increased awareness and practice you can grab the wheel, shift gears and drive yourself toward your action plan. Refer back to the previous section on saying YES to remind you how to shake loose from the excuse monster that seems to live in everyone's closet.

I won't lie and tell you it'll be easy. As they say, old habits die hard. But with some practice, and maybe a little help from your friends, you'll be surprised at how excuses fade from your vocabulary and mind-set.

NOTE: Sometimes you just don't want to do something. That's ok, too, and isn't to be confused with excuse-making. "No, I don't want to spend my weekend driving up to the outlet malls," "No, it's not a good night to meet you for drinks at two am," and "No, I am most definitely not up for planning a vacation to Canada." Being clear is a strong suit. Play it well and don't worry about what anyone thinks because of it.

If distinguishing and extinguishing your excuses seems monumental, just ask for help. That's what friends are for, right? Through thick and thin, we are there for each other. Try the above exercise with a good friend. Hide your boxing gloves, resist the temptation to flatten their bike tires when they call you out on your stuff, and thank them in the end.

GET OUT OF YOUR OWN WAY

We can be our own worst enemies, and often get in our own way. I didn't tell my parents at the time, but the only real reason I wanted to go to college was to play soccer. I didn't know what to major in because that's not why I was going to school. I asked the coach what most of the players' majors were and he told me it was Sports Management. This became my major, too.

I wasn't recruited, but was invited to preseason with all the scholarship players and a few others like me. The coach sent me a workout program for the summer; I did the program and so much more. I wanted to play soccer at college and was going to do everything in my power to make it happen.

63

To this day I am inspired to dive into adventures that are mentally and physically out of my comfort zone. If I remain in top mental and physical shape, I figure I will be ready for anything. I never want my physical fitness to be a reason I can't do something. Physical fitness is something most of us can control. No matter what your adventure choices are, you will lead a healthier life if you are physically fit.

Two weeks before school started all the invited athletes showed up for preseason. We worked out three times a day: 6am was running, 11am was skill and technique, 4pm was scrimmage. Most of the athletes knew each other from National Camp and Junior Olympics. I had none of that in my favor. I was quiet, I listened and was friendly but was secretly so overwhelmed, feeling way out of my league. I wasn't going to let the other players-- potential future teammates-- know this. After all, we were all competing for the roster of twenty-five players.

A week later, I called home and told my parents I wanted to come home. I was homesick and the feeling of being out of my league had grown by uncomfortable proportions that I thought I could no longer hide. The next day my dad drove the two hours up to Amherst, Massachusetts and sat with me in the car in the parking lot of the soccer field during my lunch break.

My dad was a man of few words. He spent a lot of time at work and I never got to see him much. I was lucky enough to train with him for my marathons, and though we didn't always talk on our runs we had an understanding of each other. We sat in the car. He drove two hours to talk to me and chances are he didn't know what he was going to say.

After a few minutes of silence he handed me a Twix candy bar, my favorite. He then told me to stick out the two weeks of preseason. "Then you can make up your mind and come home

64

if you want to," he suggested. "Just like when we start a race you always have to finish. Never quit before it's over. It doesn't matter how you do, you just have to finish what you start."

CREATING OPTIONS HELPS RELIEVE STRESS

My dad's advice was simple. I just needed a reminder. The most important part of my dad's words was that it gave me options. Any time you can give yourself options it helps relieve stress, pressure or that feeling of being trapped. It can make you see things differently. It gave me a feeling of relief that at the end of the two weeks if I still felt the same my parents would support my decision to come home.

Lunch hour was over and my dad headed back home. I went to practice that afternoon followed by five minute individual meetings with the coach for each player. Coach Banda was a tall, intimidating man. I had no idea what the meeting was about but he started it by saying, "As it stands now, if we had a game tomorrow, you would be first off the bench." I couldn't believe what he was telling me. I thought I wasn't going to make the team and here I am first off the bench. I left the office in amazement. That year I went on to start for the University of Massachusetts' women's soccer team, ranked number one in the country.

As humans, we tend to be our own worst enemy and this experience was a life-changing moment for me in my life. Never take yourself out of the game, never quit. Someone may knock you out or down, but don't let it be you! My dad may have thought that he was just giving me a pep talk but I will never look at a Twix bar the same way. When I am standing in line at the grocery store I always look down to see the Twix bar smiling up at me as if to remind me to never give up.

DO THIS: Define Your Own Options

If you're in a rut or feeling stuck, options can save your tail. Contingency plans always help you feel better, like safety nets that catch you when everything is falling all wrong.

It might seem really simple, and it may even be something you already do subconsciously, but writing them down to see in black and white is a whole different story, allowing you to see that there's a sure-fire way to help you feel more confident about leaping off the cliff, knowing you have several options to count on.

Go ahead. Write down plan A, plan B, plan C. My guess is that you'll be instantly relieved just knowing there are options, which will free up your energy to move forward and make it happen.

DON'T WAIT FOR THINGS TO HAPPEN. MAKE THEM HAPPEN.

To make change, to motivate, to lose weight, to stop smoking, to eat healthier, to find a new job, to start a business--the first step is the hardest. Don't wait until Monday or the New Year, do it now! In fact, some of the other steps are pretty challenging too. It takes constant motivation--coupled with focus and passion to move forward.

There will be times where you'll encounter speed bumps and obstacles and feel like you are making no progress, but the more passionate you are about what you are doing, the less you will see those obstacles.

Don't lose sight of what you want. Constantly keep your focus, and make adjustments as necessary. Sometimes it is just small steps, sometimes a stride. The small steps are your daily actions and they mount up. Be patient, remember a few small steps often equals one large step.

Don't be afraid to take a step back in order to move forward, but don't let this step back derail you. If this happens, brush yourself off and throw some mud on your face and get back in the game. If it was easy everyone would do it.

When I was younger, I had a dream of being an actress. I had no formal training, no experience. In fact, I was too shy to try out for school plays and had an awful memory, so there was not a chance of me remembering my lines. But I would hear of stories where some producer plucked someone off the street and made them a movie star. I was convinced that was going to happen to me.

As you might guess, it didn't. So I followed my more realistic goal of working for a big company and later making the best decision of my life to move to Key West to follow my dream of living on an island, owning my own business and having a dog. Once I was on the "right path" of living my more authentic life, I felt like I was creating my own happiness. I was no longer dependent on anyone else. I had made my dream a reality.

As the next years flew by, I remembered how I wanted to be an actress. Still believing that I could make things happen, and not wanting to give up my current life of what I was doing and where I was living to pursue that original dream, I decided I was going to bring that dream to me. Without any training, experience or contacts, the chances of being an actress where slim unless I wrote, directed and starred in my own movie. I also knew that if I wrote it myself, I would have a better chance at remembering my lines. So that's exactly what I did; I wrote a two hour movie, followed by a half hour sitcom.

Without realizing it, one of my marketing campaigns at work morphed into a reality show. We had written our first treatment for a production company. Before I knew it, entrepreneur and celebrity Pat Croce and movie director Tim Chambers were coaching us on the reality show treatment and invited us with them to pitch the show to the Travel Channel.

Four months later we were filming our first screen test in Orlando with Pink Sneakers in preparation to pitch to the major networks. My dreams were coming true. We were dealing with a major production company who loved our concept and a celebrity who was coaching us through it. For so long, I had been all about the outcome. For the first time in my life, I was appreciating the journey.

Yes, I wanted the ultimate outcome of being an actress, but writing treatments, working with different people within the entertainment industry, filming a screen test, and pitching to networks was an incredible experience and a highlight of my life. It wasn't that I "failed as an actress" but that I enriched my experiences with film production.

Focus on the ultimate goal. As you go through life you will find you make small decisions, many times without knowing, that will eventually lead you there.

CHAPTER SIX

OTHER PEOPLE

*People who dream of something
bigger and better are good role models.*
-Andrew Shue

My life in flip flops has led me to meet exceptional people that I could never have imagined meeting. Maybe it's the combination of these exceptional people doing what they want and living where they want that makes for heightened personal interactions. Not a day goes by that I don't think about how blessed I am to have certain people in my life. Even brief interactions with "strangers" affect my life in a positive way, and I'm grateful for that, too.

Even though it's ultimately up to you to make your Millionaire in Flip Flops lifestyle actually happen, your allies will show up along the way to help make it so. Your allies are the people that have your back. You can lean on them and they will be there, solid rocks along the way. They might not always tell you what you want to hear, but for that, you can trust them.

While I don't recommend constantly putting your full weight on them, it's good to know you can if you need to. Invite them in and celebrate them as often as possible.

When my fifteen year relationship dissolved, I returned to my house after helping my ex move into her new apartment, overcome with loneliness. After all those years, I wasn't sure who I was without her. I was "just Sue."

Though Robyn left me everything except the dining table and

the artwork, when I walked in and closed the front door behind me there seemed to be an echo in my house. A week went by and I couldn't stand the echo and silence any longer. There was no love filling up the rooms, my house was empty and I needed to fill it. But how?

I decided to have a party, inviting twelve friends over for wine tasting and painting. They had no idea what the painting part was but the wine got them over.

The night before the party I went to the craft store and bought different sizes and shapes of canvases. I then painted them all a different color. When my friends arrived the next evening, the wine tasting kicked off the party. It was really nice being together, drinking a lot of really good wine and lubing them up for the painting part of the party. Everyone was asked to pick a canvas and paint something... anything. One friend painted a very detailed Dr. Suess character, another, a tic tac toe box, and another took the canvas out to my drive way and threw all different color paints on it.

The next day, I hung all the paintings on a focal wall that you see as soon as you walk into my house. It was a random collection of paintings but they were painted by my best friends and it filled my wall with love. I smiled every day I came home and walked in the door. The echo was gone.

DO THIS: Call On your Top Dogs

Who do you call when the world seems to be collapsing on you? Who do you reach out to make you laugh so hard stuff flies out of your nose? Which person is it that will wade through a flood to help shake you from your delirium and get you to higher ground, only to return the next day to mop your floors and help you salvage your stuff?

THESE are your top dogs. Remember them, honor their loyalty, scratch behind their ears often, and let them know how much you love them back.

LISTEN UP!

Listening is an important aspect of life both in business and to personal relationships. We have a tendency to not listen very well. We think about what we want to say next while we are "listening" to someone talk. If you just listen, *truly* listen for a day you will notice most people don't answer the question someone asks of them or don't hear what someone is actually saying. Or even more likely, you'll notice how often people interrupt each other. Or that you're guilty of interrupting others, too.

Listening is where growth happens. You can learn about whatever interests you from listening to other people. But most of us would rather talk about ourselves. You already know about yourself, why not listen and learn? I bet you would say you don't have an ego. So why do you feel the need to always talk about yourself? We all love to talk, to give our points of view or to tell a story, but if you are only listening to yourself you will only be as smart as you are now. Listen and learn from everyone and everything, even if all you are learning is what not to do.

A few years ago, I had the incredible experience of working with entrepreneur and celebrity Pat Croce while diving into my dream of becoming an actress. While I didn't ever become an actress, I learned and grew by listening to him. Pat reinforced in me the most important lesson that still stands solid, it is the value of people. People are a great asset. Listen to them.

Pat liked that I knew a lot of people in town and that I always kept in the loop of what was going on. The reason I know a lot of people is pretty simple, actually. It's because I *like* people, and I like networking. I don't really do it in the traditional business sense; I just get out and about and let people get to know me and am genuinely interested in getting to know them. Getting to know people is pretty easy, when it comes right down to it. My shyness doesn't even factor in because people make it so easy for me.

How, you wonder? People love to talk about themselves. The more you can let people talk, ironically, the more they will like you. People feel good about themselves when they feel someone is listening to them. They will remember their interaction with you as positive because they talked and you listened.

People that I choose to spend time with have one thing in common- they are nice. Rude, unfriendly, disrespectful people, no matter how they can help you, are not worth your time. There are so many wonderful people in this world. Use your time wisely and get to know them. Listen to them.

I have actually incorporated listening as a job at Lazy Dog. When season hits (or anytime we are busy, for that matter), I add an extra person to the schedule so that the staff can take their time with customers. There is so much more to be said about a trip where our staff can take the time to talk with and listen to our customers rather than simply collecting their money and sending them out on a kayak or paddleboard.

An added bonus is that not only do the customers feel good about their experience but sometimes in return we learn. The stories our customers share are often invaluable, allowing us to expand our perspectives of the world and enjoy our day as we go about our business.

DO THIS: What a Reporter Knows

If you want to get to know someone or find out as much as possible about a situation, try using the approach that starts with WHO? WHAT? WHEN? WHERE? WHY? and finally, HOW? They are essential interviewing tools that you probably learned in eighth grade and have since forgotten because your focus has been more on yourself than on listening to others.

No problem.

In your best reporter fashion, try to naturally insert one of these questions in your conversation and let your dialogue turn into their monologue. You'll be amazed by what some people share.

ROLE MODELS

While it's up to you to make your life be what you want it to be, there are others out there waiting and ready to help you. (Richard Branson, the creator of Virgin Air, and Madonna are two of my role models. I would love to meet them as they are amazing business people, marketers and true to living the life of who they are).

Pay attention to who you meet on a daily basis. The more you interact with others, the more you will find role models right under your nose. I was lucky enough to meet one who has been a part of my life for the last five years. His name is Tommy Taylor.

I met Tommy when a friend of mine told me about a bootcamp class on the Navy base. You show up at 5:30 am and he runs you through bootcamp for civilians. I'm all about any kind of working out, but from what I knew, at bootcamp they get in your face and yell at you; that didn't sit well with me. My friend reassured me that he is all positive, so I recruited Elisa, the only friend that would get up at five in the morning to go work out to go along with me.

We showed up to the Navy base and were put through a ringer of a workout. It was so amazing that we were both smiling the entire class as we were sweating through our exercises. Tommy was about 57 at the time and a specimen of mind and body fitness. He was aware of everyone, with a perfect balance of being commanding, gentle and quiet.

Tommy offered this training free of charge, doing it for the last eighteen years because he feels the country has an obesity problem. He believes that if we become fitter as a country, the burden on the government would lessen. He was and still is incredible. His story is incredible, too. One that makes you realize your mind and body have amazing power.

Tommy was born with severe asthma; at five years old, he almost died from an attack, and doctors told his mother he probably wouldn't live very long. Tommy heard those words and made a decision in his young mind to survive. In fact, he decided to thrive.

Tommy began to run. Every day he tried to make it just a few steps further before his asthma kicked in. "One more lap," he'd say to himself, then continued running until he couldn't breathe. The next day he'd be back for more. Eventually, he could run faster and farther than most of his peers. That's when football came along. Tommy became a champion in high school and played semi-pro in South Carolina.

"I realized how powerful the brain could be," he says. "I thought about my goal and heard it in my head. My body responded."

Tommy's body kept on responding as he rose through the ranks of the U.S. Navy. After serving his first tour, Tommy knew he had found the career for him. Tommy moved up fast during the twenty-seven years he served in the Navy, and ended with the highest enlisted rank of Master Chief--one that only one to two percent of the military achieve.

His program is more than just bootcamp. "It's about helping people re-shape their attitudes," he says. "If you change your thoughts, you change your attitudes."

Tommy is just one example of the many people whom I have been blessed to meet and become friends with--people who have made a significant impact on my life. They have opened up doors to dreams I never thought could come true, helped me obtain a healthier lifestyle both mentally and physically and helped me become more spiritual. These people are my idols and I am lucky to have them in my life. They appeared once I started breaking my routines and opening myself up, doing things I had never done before and living by the motto "the answer is *no* unless you ask."

So pay attention to the people who are around you and if you like something in someone and you don't know them, then get to know them. Surround yourself with good people. When you live your life the way you want, keep true to your values and surround yourself with like-minded people, inevitably, more like them will continue to come your way. As you immerse yourself in life you will find you have role models in your every day. Embrace them.

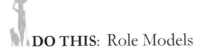**DO THIS**: Role Models

Consider your role models. Take a few moments to think of

who they are, then write them down. Go ahead. Do it now. Then list some role models in your every day life. Write down what they bring to you, then TELL THEM. Chances are they have no idea what they mean to you, and your expression of gratitude to them will only make you both feel great.

After you have made your list of role models write down what it is you appreciate about them.

Mine, for example:

Pat Croce: Entrepreneur, motivational speaker, author

- Understands the value in people.
- Is able to show his emotions but remain strong and confident.
- Is always positive.
- Takes care of his mind and body every day And s incredibly fit.
- Helps entrepreneurs open and operate businesses.

Tommy Taylor: Navy Master Chief, trains mind and body through bootcamp

- Knows happiness is a choice and makes the choice to be happy every day.
- Shows others that self-health comes first.
- Exemplifies the mind and body connection.
- Always positive but not afraid to share his own tough or stressful times.
- Volunteers.

Elisa Levy: One of my closest friends, entrepreneur, motivational speaker

- Is honest, realistic and caring.
- Chooses to be positive.
- Values people and really listens.

- Works her body every day running and in the gym.
- Works her mind every day through meditation.
- Has a love of learning and is constantly growing.

Michel Gehin: Oriental Medicine healer who saved my mind and body

- Exemplifies the mind and body connection.
- Is physically fit, always working out differently.
- Listens to his mind and body, knowing when it needs rest and providing himself with proper nourishment.
- Volunteers his time.
- Constantly attends seminars to learn and grow then shares what he learns.
- Exudes peacefulness.

When you look at your list of people and the qualities that you value about them, it will probably sound a lot like what you aspire towards.

In scanning the list of the people above, I realize that I value people who don't hide their insecurities, vulnerabilities and worries. They are all willing to admit and talk about them, but they choose to not be owned by adversity. Instead they are positive and supportive... every day!

They work out their minds and bodies every day, knowing that the healthier they are, the more they can give to others. They strive to constantly learn about themselves, about other people, places and things in order to keep growing, and they all have a sense of inner peace. These are all things that help keep me on my path.

When **you** do this exercise, you'll inevitably find the qualities that point towards your desired path or reassure you that you are on the right track.

CHAPTER SEVEN

LIVING WITH INTENTION

Our intention creates our reality.
-Wayne Dyer

If I could have created my dream paddleboard race, it would be down the Na Pali Coast in Kauai, my favorite place as far as life experiences and the most beautiful place I've ever witnessed so far. During my second visit to Kauai, that paddling dream came to fruition.

There were four of us who traveled to Kauai and I convinced them all to paddle with me in a seventeen mile downwind race. It didn't take much convincing, as Holly, Aranza and Liana are always up for an adventure, one of the reasons we are such good friends.

There is nothing like taking four Florida flatwater girls and putting them in six to eight foot swells for seventeen miles down the least-traveled waters of the Hawaiian islands. Not to mention that once you start, there is no turning back. The wind is too strong and with only jagged cliffs forming the coastline, there is no place to stop and rest. All the locals we met days before the race thought it was unsafe and said we were crazy.

We borrowed beginner paddleboards from a surf instructor we'd met then we signed up. The organizers were even worried about us. Are you comfortable in these conditions? Are you all strong swimmers? Will you keep an eye on each other out there? The answer to all those questions, we would ultimately discover, was "no".

Ordinarily we would have kept an eye on each other, but as soon as the race started, a big squall came in and we couldn't see anything, let alone anyone. On top of that, we were told "don't be too far away from the cliffs or you will be blown out to sea," and "don't be too close to the cliffs or you will get slammed into the rocks by the waves." What was too close or too far was different for each of us, so after the first five minutes, we never saw each other until the race was over.

I paddled about a quarter of a mile off the cliffs, while most of the other racers went farther off shore to catch more tailwind. After a few miles, I found a similar pace with a younger woman named Hannah. Together we paddled and chatted for the next eight miles, trying to chase the woman in first place about a mile in front of us. Every now and then a big eight foot swell would come and catch one of us off guard and we would fall.

When we were separated I would wonder why she was on her knees (if you paddle more than five strokes on your knees you are disqualified), but it turned out the swells were so big that all I could see was her hat and she was actually standing. In a downwinder you want to catch as many waves as possible and when I would catch them I would be smiling ear to ear, thinking "if only my parents could see what I was getting myself into now."

I tried to focus on staying on my board and as the race went on I got better and better riding the waves. Eventually, Hannah and I caught up to the woman in front. She kept looking back, which told me that she was tired and worried about us. I decided that with six miles left to make my move, I would paddle as hard as possible for fifteen minutes and try to get some distance on them. I figured Hannah would be right on my tail. For fifteen minutes, I paddled like I was in a sprint race, wanting to turn around to see where Hannah was, but paddling fast and keeping my focus forward.

After fifteen minutes, I was exhausted. I turned around and I could barely see either one of them. I was alone and in first place. That's when I started to cry. I was in the most beautiful place in the world, paddling in my dream of all dreams race, passing the cliffs of the place that held so many fond memories, the place of the "coolest thing I had ever done" to date. I spoke to the cliffs, offering my love and gratitude, feeling more alive in that moment than ever, my body covered in goose bumps.

Swells started to subside and the last five miles were flat water with a strong side wind. Flat water paddling--what I am more suited for. I opened up my lead. The finish at Polihale beach was in sight. I followed a few men who were in front of me, uncertain of which part of the seven mile stretch of beach was the finish line.

As they made their way to the beach, they would ride a wave in. One by one, their paddleboard would shoot straight up into the air. It was no different for me. A wave caught and body slammed me; my board shot straight up in the air, still attached to my ankle by my leash. I took my ankle strap off and now had a thirty yard run up the sand bank to the finish. The arches of my feet were cramped and my toes were numb as I hobbled up the finish, sobbing in unbelievable happiness.

When I crossed the finish line, my eyes caught hold of a girl sitting on her board cheering for me. I'd actually come in second. But it didn't matter. It was the most incredible experience of my life. Not only is the Na Pali Coast the most beautiful place I'd ever seen, it was racking up some points in my life of experiences.

I couldn't stop the tears of happiness from flowing as I stood on the blazing hot sand in the middle of a seven mile stretch of beach waiting for Holly, Aranza and Liana to finish. Forty minutes later, they surfed a wave in and body slammed on the beach. I started to cry again as I was so grateful to not only see them finish this amazing accomplishment but to also have such incredible friends that don't think twice about getting outside their comfort zone. Having friends to share your experiences with only makes it more sweeter.

TWO WORDS TO ADD TO YOUR VOCABULARY

I would go on to compete in this race every year. Every year I go back I contemplate buying artwork by a Kauai legend, Steven Valiere. I have no problem blowing a thousand dollars on an adventure but I can't seem to spend it on material things. Steven's paintings struck me the first time I saw them, and every year thereafter I would battle with myself, even saving money for it prior to the trip so it wouldn't seem like such a big purchase. But I always copped out.

The year of the Na Pali race I got my first piece of Steven Valiere art, a piece that money couldn't buy. It was a hand-painted trophy for my second place finish in the Elite division. I even got to meet Steven at the podium. It just so happens the Na Pali Race is run by professional surfer Evan Valiere, Steven's son. Priceless.

The above story is a lesson on how to "manifest." While I didn't exactly set a goal to do the race and it appeared to have happened rather accidentally (as did the acquisition of Steven's art!), I believe there really are no accidents and if you set your "intentions" clearly, all sorts of great circumstances will show up to surprise you.

You might already be familiar with the words "manifest" and "intention," but if not, it is paramount that you understand their meaning and concept. These words are a integral components in exploring the Millionaire in Flip Flops lifestyle.

Intention: an act or instance of determining mentally upon some action or result.

Manifest: to prove; put beyond doubt or question.

Knowing what they mean is one thing. Incorporating them into your daily life is another. How you do so is entirely up to you. In fact, the quality and caliber of your life depends on it.

My best friend Holly introduced me to these words and how they can mark your life in epic ways. We were in Hawaii, on a vacation I'd only ever dreamed about. Hawaii had always been on the top of my list but the time to go never seemed right. But then the day came. My business was steady. I had a great manager. I was free to go.

Holly had been to Kauai, the Garden Isle of Hawaii, on a soul-searching, month-long solo trip and absolutely fell in love with it, so she suggested we go there. I thought that Hawaii would be the place of romance I would visit with my partner but instead I was heading there with a friend, for myself.

Traveling 3,000 miles away from home with someone fairly new to me made me realize that my fifteen-year relationship was really over. While I was adjusting to that loss, Holly was dealing with the loss of her dad who had passed away a week earlier after a long illness. We were both in emotional places and knew this would be a trip of reflection and growth.

As soon as we arrived I had to buy a journal because the island of Kauai opened my soul and I needed to get some stuff out of my head. We prepared for our first adventure--a twenty-two

83

mile hike along the Na Pali Coast--packing tents, headlamps, food, first aid kits and a total of thirty-five pounds of other necessities required to help us be completely self-sustainable. We were fully equipped, with enough food to fuel our bodies, hydration packs and water pumps for purification to prevent contamination from the waste of feral goats and wild hogs in the streams. The first half would be eleven miles in to the Kalalua Trail on the Na Pali Coast. We would spend a couple of nights there and then venture back out.

The trailhead begins on the north shore of Kauai where the main road ends at Ke'e Beach. The Sierra Club rates Kalalau a 9 out of 10 on the scale for difficulty. This made me more nervous since I had never hiked before, never mind while wearing a thirty-five pound backpack. I had never actually enjoyed hiking, which to me was like going for a walk up a hill. There was not enough adrenaline to it. Or so I thought. Since I had not experienced much hiking, I got myself in top physical shape, the only thing I figured I could do to prepare for the hike.

By sunrise, we began our journey. The first part of the hike was straight up for two minutes under shaded trees over the rocky trail. All the while I'm thinking, "Are you kidding me? If the trail is like this for eleven miles (which translates to about eight hours of hiking) and I'm tired after two minutes, I'm in trouble."

I followed Holly and tried not to think about my heart pumping out of my chest, reminding myself that I would follow her to the end of the earth and not question it. Funny thing is, that's exactly where it felt like we were going. We continued on for about a quarter of a mile to a clearing in the trees where we could look back on Ke'e Beach where we had started the hike. Holly stopped and said, "This is where we set our intention."

"Intention?" I thought. "What's intention? Because I've never set one."

Having had a friend/spiritual guru take her on this hike a few months earlier, she explained. "Let's take a few minutes and think about what we want out of this hike." Besides the obvious for me, which was actually completing the hike, I wanted to open myself up to people and experiences. I was on a mission to live. I was at a crossroads in my personal life and feeling a bit out of control, which was new to me, new as in never in my forty-two years new.

I had to admit, being out of control was sometimes refreshing and fun. But being a boss and owner of a company, the girl who always had it together, made some people uneasy. I wasn't sure how I felt about either scenario. I figured if I could remain open, signs would come to me.

We hiked on, which was challenging, very rocky and continually shifting between ascents and descents, which takes a lot of focus and is very straining on the body. The trail was muddy and slippery in spots. After about two miles, we came to Hanakapi'ai beach. You have to leap onto boulders to get across the stream to access the beach, hoping you connect with the boulder in efforts to keep your hiking shoes and backpack dry!

This was a rest stop for hikers heading all the way in but for day hikers it was a destination. Many day hikers would turn around there after spending their day enjoying a picnic, playing along the stream that feeds into the ocean, and frolicking in the caves along the beach when the water is low. Swimming is not recommended, as there are strong rip currents. It was absolutely amazing, but for us it was merely a pit stop. We took off our packs and had a snack. I could have stayed there for hours except for the people coming and going.

After our break we moved on. From this point, we endured a strenuous climb about eight-hundred feet up. It was a quiet climb. The trail climbed straight up and out of Hanakapi'ai valley. We came to a narrow opening flanked by two giant boulders fittingly known as "The Gates."

You can feel the energy of The Gates, as if you dare to come through, you are at the mercy of the trail. The trail will test your spirituality, your intentions, your will. It may not heal you but it will open you up so that you might fix yourself if you're ready and willing. We placed our hands on both boulders on each side of the gate and catapulted ourselves through as if we were jumping off a cliff. We stopped and paid our respect to the ancient Hawaiian spirit gate keepers.

The trail switchbacks led us in and out of the day's harsh sun. We stumbled upon streams, waterfalls, bamboo fields and lush vegetation as the trail passed through the shaded forest. We clung to the cliffs that rose nearly a thousand feet above the sea in some areas, and marvel at the vast ocean and open sky. Sometimes the trail at the cliffs would be only a foot wide with a sheer drop off. At every turn I would say, "this is the most beautiful view I have ever seen," only to be trumped by the view at the next turn.

Next, we arrived at the sixth mile, Hanakoa. This was a regular stop for people going to the end because it has a big stream where you can pump some fresh water. Hanakoa Falls feed the stream. You can hike to the falls but it is a little over a mile round trip and the trail is said to be unkept and often difficult to follow as rain washes out sections of the trail. So, we didn't explore the falls. Our focus was to arrive before sunset so we could have sunlight to set camp.

There weren't many people at this stop. Some tents were set up in the valley because this is an end stop for some and for others an overnight stay to break up the full eleven miles over a couple of days. We pumped enough water for our hydration packs, which were almost empty, and headed out.

So there were The Gates just after Hanakapi'ai at mile two, which were a physical reality, and then there was the wall, a mindset we couldn't escape, which after nine miles and six hours, we both hit. We had just traversed an eroded fifteen hundred foot section of the trail where the path had become no longer recognizable. This was so much harder than a marathon. Marathons last three or four hours, but to be physically active doing the same things for six hours is mentally and physically exhausting. We took breaks often but at one point we were so exhausted that we leaned against trees to take the weight off our backs. It was as if the trail knew exactly when we couldn't take one more steep step in the upward direction as it would switch back to a steep, downward path.

The last two miles of the trail, Red Hill, turned to dirt and clay so dry and dusty that if there wasn't the beautiful view of the Pacific Ocean you would think you were in the deep Southwest desert. Our descent down brought us to mile ten and our home for the next few days-- a green grass bluff perched on a cliff over the wild ocean. We unloaded our packs, set up our tent, packed some dry clothes and headed across the last mile in to the beach at Kalalua, a one mile stretch of beach with only a few people to be seen.

We bathed in the stream, explored the freshwater caves and made it back to our campsite at sunset. It was one of the most amazing sunsets I have ever seen (and I live in a place of amazing sunsets). We boiled water with our jet boil and cooked astronaut type food. It didn't matter what we were eating because between the sunset and eventually the stars, I was happier than I had been in years.

As I laid on the cliff watching the stars, I was so proud of myself for completing the hike, which was way outside my comfort zone. I probably would not have done it without the confidence and reassurance of Holly. But as I fell asleep that night, totally exhausted, my body sore from head to toe, I wondered how the hell I was going to get out.

Fortunately, I had a couple of days to address that concern. The next two days we did day hikes into the valley, picked and ate fresh fruit, took naps by the waterfall, wrote in our journals and met amazing people. I felt a peacefulness that I had never felt before.

Pretty much anyone you meet at the end of an eleven mile hike is going to be an interesting person. The old Sue would have not opened up to the people of the trail but with Holly, we met everyone, which made the trip that much more fun and interesting. She was into experiencing the true life of the trail one hundred percent, as she does with everything else. With her open attitude and my own personal intention of being open, we enjoyed the rewards of our efforts and soaked up the beauty of being in a part of the world with the amazing people there.

Besides the hikers who come in and camp a few days, there are some people who "dwell" in Kalalau. There was a chef, a hippie girl that makes slippers from palm fibers, a gypsy who makes shell jewelry... these were just a few of many interesting characters. They basically live off the land, and when hikers leave the trail it is common for them to leave their unused food, matches and such for these people. These people don't have much but they are extremely hospitable. They'll offer you their homemade wine, a fish dinner caught off the beach, fruit off the trees and an escort to the most beautiful waterfall that you would never have found on your own.

We had an amazing few days because we didn't have an itinerary or agenda. Time did not dictate where we went, when we slept, when we ate. We just went with the flow, which allowed us to truly live in the present. Despite my aching body, I felt better than I'd felt in a long time, which set the tone for everything else that followed in my life from that point on.

There is so much power in your intentions and your ability to manifest them. Once you start incorporating this concept into your daily life, a world of wonderful opportunities, experiences and people will flood your life.

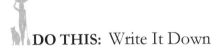

DO THIS: Write It Down

The journal. It really DOES help. Go on and get yourself a notebook and get writing. You don't have to be the next best-selling author to write your thoughts out on paper. You just have to be willing to write down what comes up and have some sort of discipline to do it regularly so that you actually get somewhere with it.

If you aren't sure where to start, that's ok. Take a deep breath and let whatever is on your mind in the moment find the page. Maybe you have a burning list of your own intentions you want to write about, or need to vent about a situation that feels off at work. Anything you write is ok, and will reveal more to you as you go.

GRATITUDE ABOVE ALL ELSE

The thing that rounded out my new outlook on life was gratitude. Gratitude is something you want to express in every day: gratitude for the bigger things such as your health, love, a friend, your job and also the smaller things, like the smell of the jasmine bloom in your front yard, or the delicious taste of your coffee. Say it out loud and more importantly, write it down.

You can have gratitude for the things you see, feel, touch, or for something that has happened in your day. You can even have gratitude for things that haven't happened yet. When you start taking stock of what you are blessed with in your life, that sense of appreciation begins to pervade, along with the idea that anything truly is possible.

DO THIS: Your Gratitude Journal

This exercise is actually pretty easy; the effort is minimal and the reward is huge. Take a journal or notebook and simply spend a few minutes before going to bed and recall your day, highlighting any of the positives in your mind. Write them down. I like to aim for at least five.

They can be really simple, like the sound the palm fronds make outside your window, a friendly exchange you had with a stranger, the hot shower you took after a long day of work.

Write down your "persons of the day."

This exercise in gratitude is important to incorporate into your every day, especially if you are feeling low. By doing it you will see how much you actually have to be genuinely thankful for.

End every day with your gratitude journal. It will help you realize how amazing your life is and will open up your heart to so much more.

CHAPTER EIGHT

TRUST THE PROCESS

I'd rather regret the things I've done
than regret the things I haven't done.
-Lucille Ball

The creative process involves a lot of dreaming, a kind of big-thinking approach. If you let your limitations determine your creativity you will fall short. You want the largest canvas you can imagine. Think unlimited resources, unlimited funds. Don't let the word "no" ever enter the room when creating and dreaming. You want yourself and others to be in a completely free-thinking environment where being told "no" is never an option.

Once you visualize your ultimate final creation, you can then work backwards and figure out how you can get there with your resources and funds. Think big, then figure out how to make it happen.

AN OLD DREAM REVIVED

I never lost my dream of working in the entertainment business and, twenty-five years later, it arrived, albeit in an entirely different form. My longtime close friend Peter (who I always seek out for business advice) is one of the most brilliant business and marketing minds I know. We created a reality show based on my business. I told Pat Croce about the show and he suggested I come down to his bar and meet some Hollywood movie executives that were in town for the weekend. Peter and I headed to the Rum Barrel, where it was too loud for any sort of talk. We handed Pat the show proposal and left. Two days later we had a contract from Pat and his movie guys to develop the show called Paycheck in Paradise.

CHALLENGE YOUR INSECURITIES AND MAKE THEM WEAKER

After what felt like a lot of waiting, Pat set up a meeting with the Discovery Network. Pat wanted Peter and me to present the show to the network with him and TV executive Tim Chambers. I quickly refused, claiming I was "not good at that kind of stuff." To which Pat simply responded "Have you ever presented a reality show to a network before?" "No," I said.
He asked, "Then how do you know you are not good at it?"

While I fumbled around trying to explain that I wasn't good at talking in front of people, Pat put his foot down. He didn't want to hear any more. He was set on the fact that the best people to present the project are the people who came up with it. When you are talking about your own project the passion and excitement can't help but come through. We would be presenting it all together.

DO THIS: Name Your Top Three Insecurities

What are the three things that get you shaking in your flip flops? Heights? Public speaking? Shopping malls? Airports? Quick, write them down.

Now think about how these fears affect your everyday life, and the choices you make to avoid them. How would it be if you

WEREN'T driven by these insecurities? What if they didn't bother you at all? Would your life look any different?

Now that you have written them down they are weaker than they were. The more you can tackle your insecurities the less of an insecurity they are. Tap into your competitive nature and beat your insecurities.

Now, I have a lot of insecurities, but the more I am aware of them the less they seem to bother me. That being said, the one I still struggle with daily is my shyness. On one hand I was living a dream experience, on the other hand I was dealing with my greatest insecurity. Oh, how the duality of our lives makes for great living!

So here I was, out of my element, about to speak in front of the top executives at the Discovery Network. There were two things that got me through that day. The first was knowing how disappointed I would be with myself to turn down an amazing opportunity. The second one presented itself at lunch right before the meeting.

For the last month we had worked through countless emails and phone calls on our presentation. We had sectioned off the presentations so each of us had our part. To sound as professional as possible, we had to memorize it. There would be no reading anything from notes. We decided to run through the presentation for the first time together in the restaurant prior to the real pitch. Tim was to go first with the opening. Then my part, followed by Peter getting into the details and then our anchor Pat wrapping it up.

Tim had pitched hundreds of shows. He was confident and likable. When he began the pitch, I was in awe of how good he sounded. How could they not buy the show? I thought. Then he stopped. There was silence for at least a minute, which is a long time during a presentation. I looked around at everyone, wondering what was going on. It turned out Tim had lost his train of thought. But then he picked back up and continued in amazing fashion.

Seeing a seasoned professional go through that, even though it was only at the restaurant, put me at ease. It gave me a strange confidence. We walked over to the Discovery building, which has a huge open lobby with dinosaurs and other exhibits. I felt like a little kid.

We waited almost an hour past our appointment when Pat finally said he was ready to leave. Waiting this long was disrespectful to anyone. I saw this potentially incredible experience go out the window. The only part of me that was happy was the shy girl who wasn't going to have to speak in public. Just then we were told to head up to the top floor, where we pitched our show to four television executives. It went incredibly well.

They were so nice and not what I imaged "people in the business" to be like at all. When it got to the question and answer period after the rehearsed pitch, it was so much easier to be natural and let my passion for the show come through.

TURN A "NO" INTO A "MAYBE"

Though they genuinely liked our show, they eventually turned it down. That didn't stop Pat. He teamed up with a production company called Pink Sneakers out of Orlando. He wanted us to work with them on developing the show.

At the meeting, the friendly staff of Pink Sneakers took us on a tour of their facility. It was a high tech, creative, imaginative office building. The president of the company had gotten the staff skateboards so they could easily get around the long one story building. I was in heaven. They put us under the hot lights and in front of the camera to get some footage.

I had been living and working in bathing suits and tee shirts and had no idea what I should wear to a corporate office. I can remember walking into Banana Republic and asking the sales girl for a "corporate casual" shirt. It was such a nice shirt that I would only wear once. I sweat completely--and I mean completely--though my shirt, on camera. So much for this easy-going girl who was selling the laid-back lifestyle of Key West. It was gross, I was gross. Let's just say that part didn't go so well.

Regardless, I was in a dream world. I have always had an infatuation with the television and movie world. I thought it would be cool to be an actress. We bonded with two of the women at Pink Sneakers, Jen and Susan, who were nothing like what you would imagine production executives to be like. They took us out to lunch before we flew home.

DON'T GET BLINDED BY THE LIGHTS

It's important not to get too enamored with any part of your process and remember what the real reasons are that are keeping you in it. Success is definitely something to strive for, but not at the cost of losing what's authentic to you.

Over the next few weeks we worked at creating the general layout of each episode of the reality show. Although we bonded with the girls we still didn't seem on the same page in the writing process. We were keen on keeping the Key West lifestyle true to itself while they were more interested in creating a hit TV show. We gathered up the nerve and told them during one conference call that we didn't like the direction they had taken. There was a long and awkward silence. Peter and I were nervous, but they eventually opened up the door to talk, helping make our working relationship grow into a very open dialogue, which further supported the creative process.

The show is still in the hands of a production company, somewhere. Maybe one day it will hit the airwaves. I don't think it's over.

WHEN THE PROCESS FEELS LIKE THE DOGHOUSE

Sometimes the process doesn't feel so good. It's so important to remember that growing pains are part of process and it's not always a smooth and easy ride. It's even more important to do your best to ride out these times as best you can, breathe deep, stay honest, and be positive.

My business with Lazy Dog has more than its share of tough times in its evolutionary process. We started with a couple of really solid years but then tried to grow too fast. We were unable to pay ourselves, investors wanted out, and we were taking cash from the profitable kayak business and paying off our debt just to literally stay afloat. The housing market took a plunge, our homes (two each!) were being foreclosed on, and we were cash poor.

While trying to manage this growth and juggle all our difficulties, my back gave out. I was laid out for three weeks and every doctor I visited told me I needed surgery. To make matters worse, my dog Molly died of cancer and Camillo, Dave's original Lazy Dog, died of old age.

But the hardest part of it all was that I was constantly at odds with Dave, my soul mate, best friend and business partner. I guess it was just easier for us to blame each other rather than look at the failure we faced as our own. This went on for a few years.

96

In 2008, after we had been in business for five years, Dave said it was time to sell. He wanted out. I, on the other hand, had no intention of selling. That job was what I did, and although times were tough I still enjoyed coming to work.

Dave had been very clear when we decided to go into business that he would give me five years. I never imagined that after five years that he would want to sell it, but he did. He was ready to leave town and move on. Our battles heated up. We would try to be fair and listen to each other but the anger, hurt and resentment overshadowed any compromise and compassion. We were both struggling in our personal lives and we continually blamed each other. We both became someone we didn't like, we said things to each other that should never have been said. It was an emotionally charged time. It was sad.

I eventually gave in and we put the business on the market. Soon after, a couple from Vermont wanted to buy. I was miserable and depressed, and felt sick to my stomach as I went through my workday. It must have really showed, because one day the manager of the marina came by and asked me what was wrong. After I told him, he gave me some sage advice that helped pave the way for the rest of my future.

INTUITION: WHEN YOU AREN'T SURE, GO WITH YOUR GUT

It seems so simple, but his advice to me was to spend a few days with the mindset that *I am selling the business*, then spend a few days with the the mindset that *I was not selling the business*. I went from a few days of being miserable to a few days of being happy. It was clear to me what I needed to do.

I sat Dave down and told him I wasn't going to sign. He broke down; this was his way to move on and I just squashed it. I felt awful. He felt awful. Nasty words and guilt flew all around but neither one of us was willing to back down.

FAITH

An outstanding pattern in my life is the belief that everything will work itself out, even if I didn't always know how it was going to. As a business-minded person I would usually try to figure everything out or create new situations, different opportunities, but now I was out of ideas, and didn't know where to turn. Dave had options. He could sell his half to an unknown person, he could walk, or he could stay. It seemed like miserable times were ahead.

Although I had thought of everything, I never expected the blessing that followed. A retired couple, Gary and Cindy, to whom I sold my first kayak to in 2003, made me an offer that was too-good-to-be-true. They were part-time residents in Key West and had invested money in the marina with hopes to help the owners expand. They were always supporters of Lazy Dog, referring renters and buying shirts for their friends. They are the type of people that brighten your day just by seeing them. They knew of my situation, the potential sale of Lazy Dog and offered to buy Dave out. A few weeks later it was done. They owned the other half of Lazy Dog with me.

But then the truly unexpected happened. They offered me their half of the business, at two thirds of the price they bought it for and would let me pay them back over ten years no interest. I still cry just thinking about this. Gary and Cindy are amazing people and are a big reason why I am where I am today. It's not something I ever would have imagined could happen, and that's just what I'm talking about. You don't have to know *how* it will work out. Just know that it will.

It was the end of an era for me and my first ten years in Key West. Although I had persevered through some very tough times, it was at the cost of my best friend. I was both very sad and incredibly relieved.

DO THIS: Overwhelm And List Making

Just so you know, there are definitely times when you need to cut yourself some slack. There is a difference between making excuses and being so overwhelmed you can't seem to move forward.

Some people, even motivated people, will lose their motivation when they get overwhelmed. When this happens, make a list of everything you need to do. It may lessen your motivation, but it may be a good starting point to get you past the place you got stuck.

After making your list, pick the one thing you have been dreading to do and do it first. I promise you, by doing this, you will feel the stress beginning to lift. Hopefully you will see the light, find your momentum and get moving in the right direction. Even if it's the only thing you end up doing that day, you will finish the day by feeling that you got something accomplished.

CHAPTER NINE

THE MIND/BODY ATTITUDE

Your body and mind support each other.
Your body helps turn what you think or dream
up into results. -Bruce Lee

There is a saying about how you can't always control the circumstances of your life but you can control your attitude towards them. The problem is, often our behaviors are so ingrained in us we might not even realize our conditioning to behave a certain way. Behaviors can act like instant reflexes, becoming a part of our mind and body make-up.

When you tune into this hugely important arena of your life, you'll start to see that you **can** control at least this part of your life, which ultimately will have a more positive affect on everything else. You have the power.

CONNECT THE DOTS

There are lots of ways to use your mind and body to change your ways. Be aware of where you are and where you want to be, and the mind and body will get you there, because the mind and body are connected in everything you do.

It was never so evident to me until my mind and body gave out. With combination of my relationship ending, my business crumbling, my dog dying, losing my best friend and business partner, the real estate market bottoming out and my back problems laying me out, I felt like the prime subject of a bad country song.

It was all so overwhelming. I had to switch my thinking and shift my attitude. I made my list and started with the most important thing, myself. I had to get myself healthy. People around town spoke highly of Michel Gehin, an alternative medicine doctor. I had never experienced this type of medical help or knew much about it; I only knew I didn't want to have surgery, I wanted to be healthy, I was desperate: I would try any thing.

Michel would ask me questions while working on my body. I told him I knew I would never run again and that I just wanted to be able to stand without pain. He replied very matter-of-factly that he could get me running again. "Ok," I said, "but I know I will never run a marathon again," to which he said calmly in his French accent "If that's what you want we can get you there."

He prescribed weekly visits for me for the next month, then every other week, followed up by every third week, which would complete our sessions. "What?!" I figured I would be seeing him for the rest of my life!

Over the course of twenty plus years I had been going to a chiropractor once or twice a week since the age of sixteen. This guy was going to cure me and that's it? I had no money at the time but I decided I would make my sacrifices so I could pay the fee. (It's interesting when you think you can't afford something. If you want it badly enough you find a way). I told myself since I was scraping to pay him, I would do everything he said. I needed to get myself better before I was able to handle the other issues in my life. If I wasn't healthy and in a good place, I realized there was no way I'd have the energy to deal with my partner or business. It had to start with a healthy **me.**

It was a slow start with Michel, which was my fault. I didn't understand the mind/body connection. Once I started to open up with Michel and answer the questions he was asking while working on me, my healing "miraculously" sped up. Michel became my safe place; I opened up and he was able to help me

102

put my emotions in a place I could understand. I had to recognize that "I am not my emotions". With this understanding, I facilitated the healing of my body.

Two months later I was running five miles a day, three days a week. My back felt better than when I was twenty years old (though my back was pretty bad then, too). Waking up and feeling no pain was new to me and this was a place I wanted to stay. From that day forward my physical health would be of utmost importance.

When tackling any issues, be sure your mind and body are healthy beforehand. You can't take care of problems or people if you can't take care of yourself. When you are sad, you start searching for anything or anyone that can help. For the most part, you are the only one who can help, so look within yourself first, and remain open. It was in the saddest times of my life that I found the people and things that positively impacted my life the most.

DO THIS: The Mind/Body Scan

On a scale from one to ten, how do feel your physical health rates? Is that neck pain limiting your ability to think clearly? Are the extra fifteen pounds making it impossible for you to feel confident? Is your energy so low you have no drive to do much at all?

What about your mind? Can't stop obsessing over your ex? Do you keep replaying the argument you had with your mom five years ago? Not sure how you're going to ever get past (insert situation here)? What are the issues that seem to plague you? Write them down, and if possible, put them in order of priority and attend to them accordingly.

There is a world of help at your fingertips. You must be willing

103

to open up and make yourself vulnerable while courageously seeking it out. Healers, health practitioners, life coaches, nutritionists, personal trainers, yoga instructors, therapists, and good ole fashioned friends can help you.

TUNE OUT THE INNER WHINER

The mind and body aren't always on the same page. This is no more clear to me than at 5:30 am when I drag myself to bootcamp. I want to be there but my body doesn't. Coach Tommy Taylor will help shift our thinking. He gets our body moving quickly and tells us "think fast, move fast." It gets you going.

Half way through a bootcamp run we stop to turn around. While we are exhausted doing our pushups Tommy will tell us to "forget about all we just did, erase it from your mind." We refresh and focus on getting back.

The mind can help the body and sometimes you will have to call on the body to help the mind. When you are in a funk mentally, go out for a run or do some sort of exercise and physically exhaust yourself. You will find your mind doesn't have enough energy to be negative or angry when you return, and you boost your endorphins in the process, too.

MEMORIZE THIS: MANTRAS FOR THE MIND

There are so many things that play a part in our daily mood; our past, future, present, food, alcohol, sleep. The more you pay attention to your thoughts, feelings, intake and actions, the more control you will have over your emotions and mood. Just as important as the food you eat are the thoughts you think. If you sit and think about something awful, you will notice that your body starts to feel it. You may even start crying. Your mind doesn't know what thoughts are real and what are made-up worries of the future. Feed your mind only positive thoughts.

Consider the many messages we tell ourselves on a regular basis. How much of it is actually helpful, positive, and true? How much of it is limiting, fear-based, self-deprecating? There are thousands of mantras we can fill our millionaire minds with, and you can be sure they will leave you feeling uplifted, optimistic and energized. Here are a few pulled from my own daily dose of reason:

Open up. We tend to be cautious of people who question us and are much more comfortable with people who share our beliefs and agree with us. Why? Because it's a secure feeling. But it is the people who bring us conflict, questions and debates that can help us grow. They make us uncomfortable by questioning us. It gets us thinking. Sometimes we may never question ourselves. Or maybe we were taught it all wrong, or maybe we adopted our belief theory or behavior from someone else. As long as it comes in a non-confrontational way and we don't get defensive, we can see it for what it is and mull it around and possibly learn to see and understand things from a different perspective.

Those that can see something from multiple angles, whether they believe that view or not, tend to be truly intelligent. Try to be patient when challenging people that come into your life. In fact, all people that come into your life are there to bring something to your table. So be patient and understanding and open to learn. Closed minded people are boring. Don't be one of them.

I was never open to alternative medicine. I was more comfortable with going to a chiropractor every week for the rest of my life, not curing my back problems but fixing them temporarily. When I got desperate, I tried anything and everything, which lead me to alternative medicine and Michel. The exercises he prescribed were yoga-type stretches, and he recommended friend and instructor Sophia, who runs her own studio. Sophia has great energy and was very attentive to my weak back and in guiding me through the classes. Yoga became a comfortable place, especially throughout all my upheaval.

During this time, my old friend Tara became a yoga instructor at Sophia's studio. While chatting one day, we decided to merge the yoga into the paddleboarding. This became a wonderful new addition to my Lazy Dog business and brings in great energy and a whole other clientele. Great things can come from desperate times. Be open and let the magic work.

Never quit. Once you start something, finish it, then move on. Don't give up. If you give up, not only do you feel like crap but it gives your competition an advantage. If you quit you will always consider it an option.

Quite honestly, I race against some people who have dropped out because of the conditions. I know going into races that I have an advantage over them because they could get stuck in their head and actually quit. It's only a mental advantage, but it's still an advantage. I've raced in races where the waves are over my head, the wind is blowing at my side and I get tossed off my board over thirty times. I've been hit on the head with my board after getting thrown off and then proceeded to get sea sick, all while I had the flu. When I finished, all the other racers were standing around saying it was the toughest race they have ever raced. I was so caught up in my exhaustion that I felt like I was the only one struggling. There was something very comforting knowing others were struggling and that I made it through.

Make yourself happy. If you want to be unhappy then I will give you this advice: try making other people happy. It's impossible to make people happy. You will make yourself miserable trying and you will fail. Making people happy is not your responsibility. Just take care of yourself, do what brings you happiness and don't let others be responsible for your happiness.

Furthermore, don't let your happiness depend on anyone else. That's not to say doing something that you know will bring joy to someone you care for is out of the question. If it makes you both feel good, then go for it. Just don't have any expectations about it and you'll all be better off in the long run.

Don't waste your time. Be in one hundred percent. When I was in tenth grade I joined the track team. I thought it was cool and my friends were doing it. Because I was a natural athlete, I didn't have to work too hard to get by in a race, so I hardly went to practice.

As the season went on my teammates were getting better than me and I was struggling. I had an epiphany: I remember as if it was yesterday. I was jogging around the track to warm up and realized the only one I was hurting with my laziness was myself. I wasn't wasting anybody's time but my own. I should do something else, like go home and watch General Hospital, I thought, or I should train.

One of my favorite things about my old business partner Dave and my friend Holly is that they are all in, giving one hundred percent even when they don't want to. I believe they were put into my life to teach me this. I have learned that it is the only way to live. I believe this was a message I have been sent over and over again in my life and now that I have embraced it my life is much happier.

We can't always do everything in exactly the manner we'd like so when something comes up that you'd prefer to skip but for whatever reason can't, just accept that you have to be there and live it up. Talk to everyone, laugh, people watch, make it fun. It's just a small amount of time in the big picture so live it up.

You might just find someone you like or actually have fun.

Be prepared. More luck comes with being prepared. Maybe you are one of those people who try all the time but don't have any luck, but your friends seem to have luck following them around. In a way, luck is planned. Lead from your head and get yourself in mental and physical position. Create all you can and you will be ready when the opportunity or luck presents itself. It might not come in the form you imagine so be open to what's presented. Be ready. You can't wait on random luck. You have to be prepared.

Be passionate. Without passion there is no fun. You want to make sure whatever you do, you love and want to do, every second of your life should be lived with passion. If you are stuck trying to live passionately in a day-in, day-out job then it's probably high time you moved on.

Let go of expectations. Expectation will set you up for disappointment. Having any expectations of other people isn't fair to them or you. Most people won't live up to your expectations so you might as well drop it and save yourself the heartache. One of my best friends used to get me so fired up because he always hummed and hawed at doing me a favor, even if it was something simple like driving me to the airport or borrowing something. I finally realized that is just the way he is. But if I ever got in a jam and I really needed him, he would be there without a doubt. I learned from him that I needed to loosen my expectations to have happier friendships.

DO THIS: Mantra Makeover

What are the messages you tell yourself, day-in, day-out? Do they work? Do you really believe them? Are there any that you could replace? What new ones would you add to the ones that are helpful? Don't just think about it. Write it down, now.

DREAMS AND THE SUBCONSCIOUS MIND

Who says you can't get any work done while you're sleeping? Sometimes your mind is on overload and the messages don't come through very clearly. But if you tap into the language of your dreams, you will find there are many messages for you, and they often hold the key to your most perplexing life circumstances.

The first few weeks I was living alone I would have crazy, vivid, colorful, detailed dreams. I would call my friend Elisa who used to be in a dream group in New York and tell her my dreams and she would analyze them. Eventually we decided to form our own dream group. Elisa picked three other people to join our dream group, all who were going through something at the time: my good friend Renee, and two people I didn't know very well- Linda, who was a psychic in town and Holly, who, at the time, I knew only from my bootcamp workout class in the morning.

Every Tuesday we would meet at Elisa's house with a bottle of wine and our dream journal. Our dream journal consisted of our dreams from the week before. We would then pick a dream to share with the group and then analyze it. Elisa led us as we were all new to dream analysis.

One of the basics in dream analysis is that you are everyone in your dream. So if you have a dream with two friends you can investigate what part of yourself that represents. If you dream of a house, the house represents your body. You may not have the same dream again and again, but you will have recurring issues come out in various versions of a dream. From here you can start to help yourself though your issues.

My dreams then had recurring themes and always included

109

water. I was either surfing or on a waterfall and it looked like I was going to get taken out by the water and then everything would be ok. Basically, my dreams were grim. It always seemed like I wasn't going to make it through and then everything ended up fine. These dreams were so vivid and went on for months.

Ironically, the day these water dreams ended was the day I bought my ticket to Hawaii, where I was going to hike and surf with Holly from dream group. The fact that the dreams stopped seemed like a sign. It was as if every night when I went to sleep my subconscious was telling me to go to Hawaii and get in the water. I knew my first trip to Hawaii was going to be powerful.

It was a very intimate group to have with strangers because we were all sharing a part of ourselves that we wouldn't normally share with most of our closest friends. I learned a lot about myself during this time, and was able to get myself through a low point in my life fairly quickly. By dealing with my sadness head-on, examining angles and not ignoring my issues, I was able to put my sadness behind me and move on towards being happy.

VISUALIZATION

Visualization is a technique many professional athletes use and one I would recommend for you. Visualize the positive outcome of work or personal projects. If you can see it, your mind has a clear road map on how to get where you want. If you aren't sure how to start, simply close your eyes and imagine yourself as the star of your own movie. See yourself doing all the things you dream of, feeling the excitement and gratitude that comes with the realization that these things are totally available to you. Then believe they will happen. Act as if they are already on their way, not something "out there" waiting to be grasp

CHAPTER TEN

LET GO

In the process of letting go you will lose many things from the past, but you will find yourself.

-Deepak Chopra

Sometimes our best ideas, our greatest loves, and our wildest dreams are never truly meant to be. When there is so much passion behind these things, it can be devastating to let them go. But if we don't, we wind up exhausted, confused, angry, physically ill and alone. In short, our energy wanes while we clutch to the very thing we think will save us.

When Robyn and I were breaking up, I found myself angry, hurt, and jealous one minute, and totally understanding the next. I was a mess. But the turning point came when I went for a walk to help relieve the anxiety I felt about Robyn not having come home for dinner.

I ran into my neighborhood friend Brad and he invited me in. I mentioned my troubles at home. Brad had been divorced but never talked about it. He always seemed in a healthy place emotionally. He gave me some of the best advice. He said, "Do everything you can do, and if it's still not enough to save the relationship, then you will feel much better knowing that you did all you could."

And so I did. I spent the next couple of weeks doing all I could to save the relationship. I was even prepared to have only half of her love as she went through this time, which I know seemed desperate but was justified by the fact that I didn't want to lose her. The bottom line was that it wasn't enough because though she still loved me, her life was pulling her in another direction. I had to let her go.

It was such a sad day. The only good thing about it was knowing I had done all I could, making it easier to come to a confident conclusion that our relationship was over. One week later I helped Robyn move her last load of possessions into her new apartment. My back had been stiffening up over the past few weeks, which I related to all the relationship stress.

The moon was full as my dog, Casey and I walked down the alleyway back to the car. I felt the pain in my lower back release. It was one of those spiritual moments, like in the choice of letting go, I was creating the space for healing to begin. I knew at that point this was the right thing and I would be all right.

IDEAS THAT DON'T WORK

Letting go also applies to grand ideas that we think will bring on what we yearn for and make what we already have even that much better.

For a few years my Lazy Dog business was growing, and though I was also growing, I was still antsy. I had a beer with a friend and the next thing I knew we were working on another business, a handheld GPS walking tour.

We found a company in England that had the software and devices. We would create a tour with pictures, video and audio and then upload it to the GPS hardware devices. We would then rent the devices. I asked my good friend Richard to be involved. He has strong technical talent and we would need that. We had enough money to buy ten units at a thousand dollars. It was expensive.

My other partner had a contact with Pat Croce. Pat was part owner of the Philadelphia 76ers basketball team and among many things, is a notable motivational speaker. This was to be the first of a few great projects we would undertake with his support.

We were ready to take the GPS business to the cruise ships, which we saw as our main clients. Pat was friends with one of the cruise line owners and we wanted his feedback. Pat liked the idea, then asked if we wanted this to be a business or a hobby. I quickly responded "Business. I have enough hobbies."

A few months later Pat invested in our company and we bought fifty units. The units didn't work and we were out a hundred thousand dollars. I felt sick to my stomach. It's one thing to lose your own money but to lose someone else's was sickening. Pat halted everything for two weeks. He wanted me to think about where to go from here. I mapped out a new plan and presented it to him. We decided to move forward.

I think it was the competitor in me that wouldn't let go. I wanted to at least get Pat's money back for him. We continued on for two years, increasing the business enough to cover expenses but not giving ourselves a paycheck.

Pat eventually shut the business down. I had failed many times before but was able to see them as experiences and lessons, but this failure came at the expense of others, involving Pat's money. I was devastated. There was part of me that was happy the doors were closed but the feeling of failure weighed heavily on me.

The reason I share this with you is to let you know that "success" isn't always what it appears to be on the outside. Many of my Lazy Dog customers think I have an amazing life and I truly do. It is a life I have worked hard for and have paid my dues with some pretty major lessons in letting go as well as letting the chips fall where they may.

Though I've had some heartache, like the two stories above, and while I've had my moments of being flat out on my back, quite literally, for weeks on end, letting go has always created more space for me to keep moving forward, often times with new ideas.

Typically, these ideas have all sprung from a place of passion. Before Dave and I opened up Lazy Dog, we tried a few other ideas to go into business together. We thought about what we were passionate about and came up with two things--wine and running. We would spend our nights at a place called The Grand Vin, a wine shop on Duval Street. It was like going to someone's house with an amazing wine collection and sitting on the porch as people you know came in and out. We would drink some nice bottles and seemed to have no trouble getting up at 6am to go run nine miles around the island. We were young.

Our first venture was going to be called NeHi (after the old grape drink that doesn't exist anymore). It would be a wine shop on the water. We would carry wine and specialty beers. We soon realized this business would make us alcoholics so we dropped it.

Our second idea was called RTI which stands for Running Tours International. We thought we were brilliant. We run to workout every day, so wouldn't it be great if we got paid for it? We got this business up and running pretty quickly after creating a logo, which is always fun but takes forever. I pitched the tour to the cruise lines that we were already working with for our kayak tour. The head of shore excursions for Carnival asked me "Are you trying to kill my guests?" That was a clear no. So we focused on the local business, getting brochures printed up and making rounds to the guest houses. I would get one person every few days.

I quickly realized that I was getting fifteen dollars to run someone around Key West while giving them a tour and running at their pace, which was usually slower than mine. For all you runners, you know how hard it is to run at someone else's pace. Your stride shortens, your hips stiffen up and you exert more energy running slowly than at your natural pace. Not only did my body not like it, I got bored.

Starting your own business is exciting. The idea of working for yourself is empowering. It's easy to get lost in all the energy of it. Not until my experience with RTI did I realize that it's not the business, it's what you actually end up doing on a daily basis for your business that matters most. I didn't like running at someone else's pace no matter how much money I was making or not making. RTI was short-lived, but the lesson would prove to be very valuable to me in the future.

When thinking about opening a business or even just taking a job or getting a promotion to a new department, think about what you will be doing on a daily basis and realize the lifestyle of the job. I shared this information with a friend of mine who was being promoted. She went from a standard nine to five, Monday though Friday schedule to nights and weekends for a small raise. She couldn't make plans and never went out. Her lifestyle changed dramatically.

It's important to remember that it's not the salary or the job title, but what you actually get to do with your days that are important. If you don't like what you do, you won't like your life.

When I was a junior in college, I remember taking a great class on Sports and Recreation Management. My degree was Sports Management and I wanted to work for a professional sports team (as a back up if I didn't become a professional athlete). I loved going to games and I wanted to be in on the action. I didn't know what I wanted to do, I just knew it was an area I wanted to be around. You know, like hanging out in the dugout.

One day in class, our teacher commented that we were all after a tough lifestyle. It meant working nights and weekends, when the games are played. I had a pit in my stomach. With things I like to do on the weekends, and friends I wanted to spend time with, that simply wouldn't work for me. I lost my enthusiasm for the sports field but remained in the program since I only had a year and a half left. I figured I would take more sports nutrition classes and at least get something out of it.

Be sure to think through any change you choose to make that affects your daily life. While it may sound good on paper, think about what it'll be like to live it.

Be careful what you wish for.

IT'S JUST STUFF

I used to be one of those people that always wanted things; the new car, the nice house. Things made me happy. For a short time, anyway. All of that was about to change.

When I first moved to Key West, Robyn and I put everything into a U-Haul, and what didn't fit, we got rid of. We sold my car and kept hers and when we got to Key West we bought bikes to get us around. I hardly had to buy any new clothes it was tee shirts, shorts and flip flops every day. I didn't have those silly "keep up with the Jones'" purchases, and I didn't want them. Life was simple.

But after seven years and moving into a bigger house we had accumulated a lot of stuff. We realized how much we had when we were hit by Hurricane Wilma. The hurricane winds came with an eight foot storm surge that flooded eighty percent of the cars on Key West and ruined the first floor of many people's homes. We watched out the back door as the water began to rise.

At first, you couldn't see the pool, then all but the top of the grill disappeared, then the car was under water. The surge came quickly. We started talking about what we needed to save. It came down to our dog and ourselves the rest was just stuff (although I admit I really wanted to save my flat screen TV).

It's a crazy place mentally when you are faced with what possessions are actually really important to you. If anything, it's certainly a reminder that health and happiness are the things that make you whole, not stuff. If you don't have your health then you don't have much. Ask a wealthy person who is sick with cancer or some other life-threatening or debilitating disease. They will tell you the money and stuff mean nothing without your health.

MAKE SPACE FOR THE NEW: CREATE SPACE WITH LESS

Four years after Hurricane Wilma, Robyn and I went our separate ways. We had collected a lot of stuff over the years and what she hadn't taken, I was left with in the house, which we had to sell. I had a yard sale and let go of almost everything I owned, aside from some clothes, my work desk and laptop, and some sentimental items. I even gave my flat screen TV to my friend. It was sad and a bit sickening to see all my belongings sold but it was necessary.

I moved into a small cottage owned by my friends' mom at the back of her house. It was about three hundred square feet, with a bed, couch, TV and small kitchen. It was a cave, dark and small.

I had always needed light and windows but for some reason I felt this was where I was supposed to be. All my bills were included in my monthly rent, so without stuff, a garden to take care of and only having to write one check a month, life got simple. I actually found that I had more time in the day now

117

plus I had less clutter in my life. And with a living area that I could easily clean in an hour, my time seemed to free up. I always wanted more time and I had it now. I had less stuff and I was living more simply. I never even missed my stuff.

The next two years were an adventure: I played more, traveled almost every month somewhere, worked out more, and spent more time with my friends. I spent less money on stuff and in turn had more money to do things. I had richer experiences and took time to travel to wondrous places.

I think the only person in my life who had a problem with this time was my mom. I think she worried about me and I get that. To go from having so much, a house, a long-term relationship and the lifetime of stuff I had acquired--to living in a three hundred square foot dungeon with only a few belongings was hard on her. Not that she ever told me, but every week that we spoke on the phone she would say, "This is good for now and when you're ready you can move on." I think it made her feel better. I just knew it was what I needed: a cleansing of sorts.

DO THIS: Purge What You Don't Need Or Love

Take inventory of all the stuff you own. Now imagine packing it up to move. What would you actually box up, and what would you leave behind? Look in your closet, your basement/attic/storage unit. What the heck is in there, anyhow, and how long has it been since you've worn/used/needed it? If it's been longer than year and doesn't hold some sort of sentimental value, consider donating it.

The same goes for papers. If it can't be filed, isn't a legal document, and you haven't seen it since you last put it in your "inbox" six months ago, chances are you don't really need it.

118

Now put yourself at the hands of a natural disaster. What items would you try to save if lost to a fire, hurricane, flood or cyclone? When it all comes down to it, what matters most in your day-to-day life?

Get rid of what no longer serves you. When you do, you'll notice that you'll want to do the same in all the areas of your life, above and beyond the physical.

FINDING FLOW

When you let go of what is cluttering your life, whether emotionally, mentally, physically or spiritually, you will begin to notice that you have less of what you don't want and more of what you do. Your life will begin to flow.

Now that I have let so much go, I have more time to do what I want. You might guess that I spend a lot of that time paddle boarding. A while back, I heard about a race in Ft. Lauderdale billed as a short track, Nascar style, anything goes race. This seemed right up my alley; a short race where you can even push other people off the board. My friends Holly, Liana, Barb and I headed up Friday afternoon for the Saturday race, and in true Key West fashion we arrived for the registration party late then kept the party going until four in the morning.

We barely made it to the race, as did others who were hung over. We didn't even have boards to race with. We borrowed some boards and entered the race. We were told the rules: start from the beach, round the buoys twice and surf small waves in. The first one to touch the beach wins, and the top three from each heat go to the finals. I had seen the prizes they were giving out to the top three: an oversized beer mug. I wanted one.

I won my first heat and made it to the finals. As the final race took off, Helga who was the best paddle racer in Florida was

119

twenty yards ahead and had an easy finish for first. It looked like the battle would be for second place; I was fighting it out with another paddler named Maryanne.

The course was only one loop this time, but just before we came upon the last buoy to turn and surf into the beach, Helga mistakenly started going around the course again. Then Maryanne, who was just ahead of me, got hung up on the buoy. I rounded Maryanne, got a perfect wave and rode into the beach. I fell off my board and smacked my hand on the beach. Helga's hand smacked the beach a second later. I'd won.

I felt bad that Helga had started to go around the buoy again, so I almost told her to take the win but my crew rejected my idea quickly, telling me it was an anything-goes race and I should keep the win. That was a good decision because for the next two years Helga would go on to beat me at every race we had against each other.

At the award ceremony I was getting excited to get my beer mug and I got even more excited when they stuffed the mug with ten twenty dollar bills and handed it to me with a oversized Dakine travel duffle bag. I just made out with two hundred dollars in cash and about another two hundred dollars in merchandise for paddle boarding. I was so excited I told Holly and Liana that I would take them out to dinner on the way home. We showered at the beach and made our way to Houston's, one of our favorite stops in Miami. After a one hundred and eighty dollar dinner tab and a twenty-five dollar parking ticket, my cash was gone but I was happy. I had a new hobby and little did I know was manifesting my new life.

After that, Holly, Barb and I would travel around Florida on the weekends racing. I started watching what boards people raced and noticed that the top racers all had board sponsors. I wanted a board sponsor. I was reminded by some other racers that since my company carried a lot of different boards from several companies, I would be able to get any board at cost. I could ride anything I wanted rather than just one brand. Ordinarily I wouldn't restrict my options but in this case I wanted to be part of a team.

I contacted Jeff Archer at my favorite board company, YOLO and they took me on and sent me a board. I was on my way. They are a great Florida-based company and I like the people who make up the company. It seemed like a great fit. I spent two years racing under YOLO, having a blast traveling all over the country doing what I love, promoting my brand and YOLO and hanging with friends.

As I started doing races, I found more and more carloads of my staff and friends joining me. At times there would be ten of us at a race. Everyone called the girls part of Lazy Dog, which I loved. Though I wasn't sponsoring any of them at the time, the Lazy Dog race team formed on its own and I ran with it. Our team is a group of ten women who love to race but more importantly, have fun and laugh, all while promoting the Lazy Dog lifestyle by doing what they do.

THE ORGANIC LIFESTYLE

People notice a pack of girls going anywhere and having fun together. We take our love of the ocean, travel, Lazy Dog and each other and have fun doing what we love to do.

Over the last few years, we've raced all through Florida, the Carolinas, California, Puerto Rico and Hawaii. Everyone has begun to recognize us, and Lazy Dog, too. Paddle boarding was growing and we got in early. As it grew, Lazy Dog grew. We were paddle racing, traveling and hanging out with our besties just being us.

All that fun actually benefited Lazy Dog and our brand. We

were selling shirts and hats and developing our brand from a local Key West brand to a national brand. We were featured in a seven page spread in the national publication Stand Up Paddle Magazine, all about Lazy Dog and Key West, just because we were doing what we love. We weren't actually trying to sell anything, we were just representing the Lazy Dog lifestyle and brand. It grew organically.

At the end of one of my races, Holly and I were walking barefoot over the beach, carrying a paddle board back to the car and things all started to make sense. Six months earlier, as I was driving home from a family reunion in St. Augustine, I was struck by an idea for my second book. I hadn't even come close to finishing my first book and I had no idea that I was going to be writing a second book but my mind couldn't contain itself. I grabbed my notebook and began to write all the thoughts that were rushing into my head. It's like my angel was telling me something and I had to write it down.

The book title that came to me was "A Girl, her Dog and a Board." It was going to document my dog and me as we traveled around the country learning how to surf. We would spend time in places so we would get to know the locals, never have an itinerary and just go with the flow to see what could happen. As Holly and I were carrying the board, I realized it wasn't a book I was writing, it was the life I was going to live, and the surfboard was not a surfboard but a paddle board. This was a manifestation.

My life dream of owning my own business, having a dog and living on an island just got better. Now I travel the world with my friends to paddleboard races and while I'm there we promote my Lazy Dog brand. It all just naturally fit into place, without force or brute effort. It flows like waves into the shore.

CHAPTER ELEVEN

SUCCESS

Don't aim for success if you want it;
do what you love and believe in,
and it will come naturally.

-David Frost

For most, success is tied up in the end result. What I want to convey to you is that success is not the end result, but the little things that happen every day leading up to the end result.

Think about when you wanted a job and thought, "If I only get this job I will be happy." You get the job and then after a while you start to feel underpaid and overworked. You get a raise but then this cycle repeats itself. Maybe another new job, feelings of being underpaid, along with feeling overworked. Then a raise. Repeat.

Don't worry, this is normal, especially for those who are continuing to grow. If you are content with what you have, there is nothing really needed for change. Obviously that's not **your** problem or you wouldn't be bothered to read this book. I would guess that most people really want to succeed, but many are never really content once they reach their goals. They always want more. Which is just one more reason to be grateful for every day and all the little things that go into it.

Success that matters most is the ability to be grateful for everything you have around you in the present moment, for all you do. And if you're reading this thinking you don't have any beauty around you then walk outside, smell the air, look at the sky. Nature is an amazing thing and we are surrounded by its beauty every day. Recognizing this is part of being successful, because you can then fine tune your perceptions of gratitude, which is a critical part of truly being and **feeling** successful. Otherwise you probably won't enjoy much of any of your successes.

DO THIS: Attitude of Gratitude

Even if you haven't yet reached the long- or short-term goals you've set for yourself, consider all that has happened so far. Think about the people or circumstances that have helped you move closer to reaching your goal. Does anything or anyone stand out in particular?

What about choices you've made along the way? Can you pat yourself on the back, too? Add these things to your gratitude journal.

While it's really up to you to make it all happen, it's important to note who and what has helped you out along the way. It expands the energy around your goal, making it that much more valuable or easy to spot when you are reaching for it.

NEVER SAY NEVER

I have held the belief that the one thing I would **never** do is skydive. That's why I decided to jump out of a plane two years ago. I have never felt anything like that before. I waited around for two hours, then my instructor came over and hooked himself to me and we got in the plane. There was no turning back. We were going to jump out of a plane.

I sometimes look at the picture the photographers took of me in the plane just before I jumped. It was a look I have never seen in my eyes ever before. I was in absolute terror and I was getting into it myself.

When we shuffled to the door I'm not sure I was given a choice. We fell out and it was absolutely incredible. I was so nervous that I kept laughing, then I started crying because I felt **so alive**. My emotions were on overload, all of them, and I felt alive in every sense. Once the parachute opened I was able to relax and enjoy the ride.

My guy who was attached to me (you would think I would know the name of the guy who I jumped out of a plane with and saved me by pulling our chute) asked if I liked roller coasters. I said "Yes," so he proceeded to spin us around, one way then the other. As we were making our approach to land, I realized I was getting ill from motion sickness. Through the entire approach and landing I was throwing up on the leg of my savior. I bet he remembered my name.

Don't ever rule anything out. Just wait for the timing to be right and the experience will be priceless.

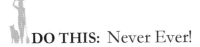 **DO THIS:** Never Ever!

What's on your "I will never list?" Make that list... then do it!

FINISH THE RACE: FOCUS, STAMINA AND FOLLOW-THROUGH

Have you ever started a project with total enthusiasm but somehow can't find your way to the finish line? For five years, I have been working on this book, putting it on the back burner as I did project after project with my Lazy Dog business. But when my business got to a point where it was running smoothly, I decided I needed to create space for further growth; two things I had set out to accomplish were my book and the franchising of my business.

These were two projects that I had spent my time and energy on and were eighty percent complete. I needed to finish them so I could create more opportunities for myself and others. Leaving them incomplete was not an option, as doing so, in my mind, would have been a failure.

When I made this agreement with myself (and truly believed it), the pieces started to fall into place. I connected with a friend of a friend who I had known for over ten years. Cricket Desmarais is a Key Wester with a Master of Fine Arts in Creative Writing from NYU. She freelances as a writer, coach, consultant and editor. We met and she took me on as a client.

I never realized that the last twenty percent of my book would be the hardest. Writing, for me, was the easy part. Giving my book to someone else to read was terrifying. In fact, I met with Cricket every Wednesday at two o'clock to talk about my book and create an action plan for the next week. After the fourth week she asked if I was ever going to give her my book. From there on in I realized that if I wanted to get this project done I was going to have to let my insecurities go and trust in Cricket and the process. I did, and soon after the book was completed.

Having a great editor is one thing but what I didn't realize was the value in her as a writing coach. Not just to help with the writers block but to help with all the insecurities that come along with writing and releasing personal experiences. It makes you feel so vulnerable, but once again so alive. The timing was right, for me, my business, to work with Cricket and for the next stage of my life to begin.

After much hard work, dedication and trust in the process, there will come a time when you realize that you have finally attained what you have set out to do. Congratulations! Success is yours. Be sure to take the time and celebrate! Too many of us forget to really take the time to applaud our efforts by acknowledging our accomplishments beyond the standard checkmark off "the list."

This might look like different things to different people. Popping a bottle of bubbly with some friends, taking that much yearned for vacation, sleeping an hour later than normal or getting up before dawn to meditate on the beach and quietly say "thanks" to all the beings out there that have helped you along the road.

We all have our way of celebrating. Whatever YOUR way is, don't forget it's an important part of the process and will help seal the feelings of success inside your soul.

DO THIS: Celebrate Your Success

Think back to your most recent success story. Did you acknowledge it? How? Now take it one step further. Think back to the success, and recall the actual goal you set before the success came. What did it look like? Was it the exact goal you intended, or did it veer off somehow, taking on a new shape? What were the steps that worked (or didn't) in making that goal a reality?

Reflecting on your process can be a fine way to honor your success, as well as help you better understand how to move forward with future aspirations. Now that you can define how it all happened, whoop it up for an hour, a day, a week... whatever it is that you do ... to help you truly feel the depth of your success.
But don't get too cozy. Resting on your laurels is definitely NOT part of the Millionaire in Flip Flops lifestyle.

But you knew that already, didn't you?

THE PROBLEM WITH SUCCESS

Even the most positive, happy people can find themselves stuck in a rut and it usually happens after you obtain a goal, whether small or grand. If you are always growing and moving forward, ultimately, you fulfill your goals. Then what? Is this all there is?

You might even feel somewhat disillusioned, begin to wonder why you don't feel as great as you might have imagined. Often times, there is a let down of working so hard to succeed and finally arriving at your grand destination.

That's when it's really important to find a new goal and keep moving forward. This will help keep you out of the rut. Fight being stagnant. Create short and long term goals constantly. Add to them and check them off once you achieve them (of course celebrating each one along the way!).

I've always been a self-motivated person. I usually know what I want and set short and long term plans to reach my goal. I always have the outcome in my mind. Although only a thought, it is a powerful thought that keeps me on target while I work through my plans.

I have had two moments in my adult life where I lost sight and didn't know what I wanted. One was after receiving "Executive of the Year" at work, when I had a sudden thought of "is this all there is?" and shortly after gave it all up to live in Key West.

Second was more recently when I had accomplished my dream of living on an island, owning my own business and having a dog. I was successful in all three and now I had time to play. Entrepreneurs dream of the day that they can have the time and money to play because they were successful with their creation. But free time is not that easy. Your mind eventually gets bored because you are not moving forward, learning and growing.

When I ran marathons my training program was always fifteen weeks long. It consisted of specific weekly goals and training, all built up to one 26.2 mile race. I would have both good and bad days of running, but I just kept moving forward, completing all my daily and weekly goals no matter how I felt.

Even with the accomplishment of finishing marathons, after every single one, the day after I was always depressed. I had dedicated the last fifteen weeks to training and now what? I had accomplished my goal; was it time to eat donuts and cookies because I deserved it? I completed my goal but didn't have anything to sink my energy into.

Imagine if you have a goal that takes years of your time and energy and you finally reach your goal. Then what? Here's what: long and short terms goals. Make them. They will help you refocus and keep you moving forward.

KEEP THE EGO OUT OF IT

About two years into my paddle racing, I competed in the Gulf Coast Paddle Board Championships in Madeira Beach. It was a beautiful Florida Gulf coast day and it would be the first time I would be paddling against the country's best paddler, Californian Candice Appleby. While it was great to place sixth in the race, the best part of the weekend was the paddle clinic with Candice a day later.

There were about twenty of us the in class, including Lazy Dogs Holly, Barb and Sandy. We showed up five minutes late and without boards. As the clinic began, my teammates from YOLO gave us some boards and the class headed down to the beach, where Candice would teach us racing "beach starts."

"Who here thinks they have a good beach start?" she asked.

Holly, Barb, Sandy and I quickly put our hands up. Candice told us to line up; when she said, "go," we were to run with our boards to the water, throw them down and jump on.

Holly went to jump on her board and face-planted over it. Barb tripped as she went to get on her board. Sandy fell over her board sideways and I fell before I even had a chance to get on my board, bloodying my knee before I even hit the water. We all got up, got on our boards and paddled out. Candice called us to come in, so we turned and rode a small wave back to the beach. I decided to ride all the way to the beach, where I promptly face-planted in front of the whole class.

When I signed up for the class, my intention was to learn from the best. Listening and watching would have been a much better option than what we'd done. It was humbling, but after that fiasco of a start you'd better believe I sat there and listened to every word she said, including her constructive criticism.

The ego is powerful and can prevent you from doing things. When you become "successful" at what you do, you tend to have expectations for yourself. This is where it all falls apart.

For example, as a competitive runner, I won most local races on the island. After my back kept me down, I was never able to return to the level I once was. So when races came around, guess who loved them but wasn't in them? Me! I was so caught up in the fact that I used to win races that I wouldn't enter if I couldn't.

This would carry over to paddle racing too. If I was out of shape I wouldn't race because I knew I could do better. But all this did was limit my experiences and adventures.

Bottom line: don't let your ego take you out of the game. It's the journey, not the destination.

CHAPTER TWELVE

KEEP YOUR PASSION

*When work, commitment and pleasure all become one
and you reach that deep well where passion lives,
nothing is impossible.*

-Nancy Coey

The best advice I ever received came from my sister Julie, and it's been the fuel for my own personal journey. "Follow your heart and everything else will follow," she reminded me during one of the more challenging times of my early adulthood. When I truly considered the depth of this seemingly cliché statement, I began to make different choices--choices that have led me to the life I now live.

I also began to take to heart a few other popular sayings and saw the effects of putting them into action: "Don't just wish it, do it" and, "Life is short so you have to make the best of every day."

Passion is defined as "any powerful or compelling emotion or feeling." It's not about calculating or strategizing, though these things certainly have their place in the road to success. It's about FEELING. What makes you feel good? What excites you? What brings you a sense of joy, of bliss, of possibility? What exactly is it that puts the get up in your go? Tune into your feelings and you will inevitably be able to use them to help you fuel your own fire.

Hopefully by now you've pinpointed at least a few of your passions and have started exploring them, or at the very least, done some serious daydreaming about them in the midst of reading this book. Everyone needs passion. There is no

MY LIFESTYLE

My dream of opening my own business--a place where I would want to spend my time and where employees would want to come to work--has come true. I work out of a shack, a hundred square foot space with a floating dock where our customers check in and where we also sell our Lazy Dog merchandise. My office is a twelve-year-old beat up picnic table under a palm tree.

The picnic table is where it all happens. We share the table with two other businesses next to ours--a jet ski and boat rental business. If the picnic table could talk, it would have much to say. From the stories about last night, to future business ideas-- the table carries it all. It's where we come up with party theme ideas, travel aspirations, and silly marketing campaigns. It breeds creativity and fun, and is a comfort zone for those that work with us.

There are days when staff even come and hang out on their day off, especially on "Sunday Fun Day," where the staff with kids hang out at the picnic table while the kids play on the floating dock and in the water.

My work has become an extension of my lifestyle, full with things I want to do and people I enjoy being around, all while being able to make a living. This is what can happen. It's possible, but YOU have to make it happen. You are unique, and must create your own lifestyle. A little passion while doing so goes a long, long way.

Without passion or purpose, the life force that propels us forward pretty much wilts. I saw this first-hand at a young age with my grandfather. Since my relatives lived in London, I would usually only see them for two weeks every Christmas. But one year, I had the great opportunity to get to know them better when my father and I went there while training for a marathon.

Welwyn Garden City is a very small town twenty miles north of London. Despite being so close to a very metropolitan city, it was very old world, and a few decades behind the times. It felt like living in the seventies.

Each day, we would walk to the store to buy whatever groceries we needed. I would walk to my granddad's and spend some time with him sitting in the living room, with only a space heater to warm the house. I hated going to the bathroom at my granddad's house because the toilet seats were so cold.

Granddad was ninety-three years old with a sharp mind and strong, albeit slow, body. Every day he would have a cup of tea and fry up his breakfast, then walk down to the shops, place a bet on the horses, smoke his pipe, enjoy a pint at the Woodman pub and then pick up groceries for the evening dinner.

Since I was visiting every day, I did all I could to help him out. I started out by doing the groceries and placing his bet each day. As the weeks went on, I realized my granddad's health had started going down hill. A few months later I went back to the States and my granddad was in terrible shape.

But shortly after, my dad flew back to England to check on him. He was better than ever, back to his routine and sharp as a whip. Then it dawned on me. I was doing all his work and daily chores. He had nothing to do, nothing to keep his mind and body active. I had been doing it all for him.

It's quite likely the reason that when people retire that their mental and physical health suffer. When you work, you have a sense of mission, you are busy and active. When you retire you still need to keep your mind and body busy, hopefully doing something you enjoy. It doesn't only happen when you're old or when you retire, you can go downhill at any age if you stop growing. If we stop learning and stop doing then we stop growing.

DON'T COMPROMISE THE PROCESS

There is a tremendous amount of energy in the present and this is where you want to live. We waste so much time worrying about stuff that never happens. If you worry about it, stress about it, hell, just think about it--you will live it. Your body and mind can't tell the difference between thoughts and reality. Don't put yourself through that stress.

In 2011, on my most recent Kauai trip, a few friends and I rented a beach house. At sunrise following our arrival, we woke and headed to the trailhead at the end of the road at Ke'e beach. Liana, Holly and I hopped on the trail and hiked for six miles at a steady pace until Hanakoa Valley Stream. It was Liana's first experience and it was having its effects. Liana would stop every so often and take a moment, sometimes yelling over the cliff "Where the hell am I?".

As we began to set our intentions, I got nervous, too. While I'm very confident in my physical ability, I remembered the last time I was on this bended trail and how it messed with my head. In fact, I think I apologized to the trail for not handling what it was throwing at me, telling it I would return a stronger person.

After eight or so hours of hiking, we made it to the big, green grass bluff where we would set up camp. Our tent was pitched just feet from the edge of the cliff. We bathed in the waterfall, had a cup of wine with our dinner and watched the sunset over the Pacific from the bluff. We didn't know that the trail was still messing with Liana, whose feet were all torn up with blisters and cuts from her hiking boots. She kept saying she wasn't sure she was going to make it out, that maybe she would pay someone to boat her out of there.

We woke in the morning and unzipped the tent to be greeted by the salty air. There was a full rainbow over our campsite. We ate some packaged oatmeal and sipped a hot cup of tea. It rained nonstop all morning. We were nearly stuck in the tent, tired but restless. We tried reading and writing in our journals but in no time the four man tent seemed like a matchbox and we all felt the overwhelming need to break out of our weather prison. We decided we had to get out of the tent and embrace the rain. We packed a daypack and hiked up valley to the ginger pools.

Once again, the people who live out on the trail amazed me. Rain or shine they are at peace in the present moment. They make the best of all conditions and God knows they have endured them all. They have barely any personal belongings and yet all they want to do is give: to guide you to beautiful waterfalls and pools, to share the history of the trail, to take you to the secret garden where they grow herbs, sugar cane, limes, cacao, breadfruit banana and lots of other fruits. If they catch or spear a fish they want you to come for dinner, if they make wine they want to share it with you, if they write poetry they want to read it to you, if they see their friends they want you to meet them. They sing, dance and create! And EVERYONE says hello and often has a story to share. It's so simple, so beautiful. The only way to experience the trail is to be open, listen, not judge, and not have an agenda or itinerary.

I was enjoying the day hikes up valley and the whole vibe of the trail so much more that year even in the rain because the trail wasn't messing with me physically or mentally. The experiences we were having with the locals of Kalalua were changing my life. But Liana was still having a hard time. When it came time to leave she was still thinking about getting on a boat. Holly and I didn't engage with her at all when she would mention it. It was as if her voice echoed off the sides of the tent but were never absorbed by either of us. It wasn't an option. We hiked in, we would hike out!

Once we got moving, life came back into our legs and we hiked out at a good pace: first over Red hill, then through the rough section about mile seven where the trail becomes unrecognizable. We zig-zagged along the sun-beaten craggy coast and back into the shady forest of mystery for miles. Liana was relying on her iPod for strength and encouragement while I took the lead and Holly trailed her as if we were her Kalalau guardians.

With about two miles left, I moved far ahead and out of sight. I got separated from Holly and Liana while taking a picture and going down a different path (although there is only one trail there are some "short cuts" along the way, usually steeper paths connecting the main trail). When I couldn't find them, I continued down to the Hanakapi'ai beach which is usually filled with people. I took a seat next to two guys under a tree close to the water's edge. Several minutes later the girls came down the trail along the stream.

It just so happened that one of the guys sitting next to me was a guy Holly met on her first trail experience. The other guy was someone we had heard all about while we were camping. He had told his friends he was going to swim in to pick up the trail, six miles along the coastline. But he never showed up. Yet, anyhow. He'd gone two miles, then camped out at the beach where we saw him for a few days. The guys shared their cacao beans and honey with us, an amazing treat since our food options had grown pretty limited. Out of habit I looked down at my watch.

"You don't need that in here," said one of the guys. "You come when you want to and you go when you want to. Do me a favor," he added, "Leave your watch on the trail."

He was probably talking figuratively but within a mile left I laid my favorite G-Shock watch on a rock, smiled and walked on. It felt good.

Not everything I learned on the trail works in my daily life but I try to be more aware of what I learned on the trail that time around. It definitely struck me how controlled I can be by time and how often we project into the future and create unnecessary stressors for ourselves that complicate what can otherwise be fairly simple (and often pretty joyful) if we just take it step by step.

A week after our trail experience, a few more friends came to stay with us in Kauai with plans to all paddle race in the Na Pali Coast seventeen mile downwinder. YOLO sent me a race board, but it got damaged by a forklift so I didn't have a board. I could have chosen to stress and worry about how I would go forward with the race, but instead, at the last minute, I borrowed a recreational board, satisfied to be in the race at all.

A half hour before the race started, my friend Sandy offered me the race board her friends lent her. I switched to the race category which gave me another hour until my start time. I took pictures and cheered the girls on as their race, the surf stock division, went off. I then chilled out under a tree for an hour, waiting for my race.

137

Hannah, the girl I had met in the race the year before, came over to say hi. Hannah told me of a film she recently saw called "180 degrees South" about Yvonne Chouinard, the founder of Patagonia sportswear. She said the movie made her think about me and Lazy Dog and our adventures of travel. Chouinard tells a story about the people who pay eighty-thousand dollars to have a sherpa do just about everything for them when they hike Mount Everest.

Chouinard says, "when you compromise the process, you're an asshole when you start out and you're an asshole when you finish."

"What you do at Lazy Dog seems so real," she offered.

It was a beautiful compliment. When she left to get ready for the race, I couldn't help but think back about our hike the week before. Had Liana taken a boat out she would have "compromised the process." She got in on her own and she got out on her own. It was authentic and no one can take that away from her.

KEEP IT INTERESTING: CHALLENGE YOURSELF

Nothing kills passion quicker than boredom. In fact, if you're bored, you're boring, so you'd better shake things up quick. Start saying "yes" to anything and everything if you have to, jot down some new short term goals, do something that scares you senseless. It'll be sure to get your heart pumping and the passion flowing yet again.

Holly and I were on the last flight out at the end of the three week stay in Kauai. On our last night, we could have just gone out for dinner and hit a bonfire on the beach, but I had different ideas. It would be the full moon; Holly had told me stories of her first hike into Kalalau during the full moon,

138

saying it was nothing like when we had been there. The energy on the trail is heightened, good and bad. I wanted to experience it.

I told her we should paddle in on our paddle boards, camp on the beach and paddle out the next day since our flight home was not until the following evening. She wasn't so sure.

After about a day and then someone else telling her it would be a cool trip, we decided to do it. I was so excited! This had always been on my mind as something I wanted to do. Holly's shoulders had been bothering her, overstrained from our paddle adventures but she was up for it. How hard could it be? This would be an easy five mile paddle compared to the seventeen miles of the race.

We borrowed the boards we had used in the race. We had our tent, food and drink all wrapped up in big trash bags and strapped to our boards. We decided to leave at five that evening. The trip would be a simple downwinder and take us about an hour and a half. We would get into the beach before sunset, set up our tent and have a delicious picnic. Easy.

We set off from the beach under a clear sky and calm water. The tricky part, we thought, would be the reef break we needed to navigate around. After that, the wind would pick up and blow us down the coast. After five minutes I looked back only to see Holly paddling harder but making no progress. At this point, I was barely paddling.

"I feel weak, my board is going nowhere!" she yelled.

If we were going to turn back, it had to be then. The wind was only growing stronger. We also had to keep moving otherwise the current would carry us to the cliffs. As we sat on our boards discussing the best choice, I became less confident that we would be able to turn into the twenty to twenty-five mile an hour winds to make it back where we started. We decided to continue on. While I barely paddled, Holly paddled harder but was still going nowhere.

I told her we could switch boards, thinking something might be wrong with her board. But Holly thought it was just her weak shoulders. The tension built and we remained quiet, worried we were in over our heads. There was no turning back, nowhere to pull over, and the waves were powerful, crashing on the cliffs. Though the scenery was incredible, we were racing hard to get to the beach before the sunset.

DON'T GET DISCOURAGED...JUST PADDLE

The sunset was amazing, though we'd hoped to enjoy it on the beach and not soaking wet in four foot seas. The trip was a mile longer than I planned, and Holly's board still seemed to be barely moving. We paddled in the diminishing light for about a half hour and finally caught a glimpse of the beach--a beautiful, one mile-long stretch of sand with huge cliffs as a back drop.

All light disappeared while we sat on our boards discussing where we'd like to set up camp. The sky was soon dark and we heard the unmistakable and unnerving sound of surf crashing. It made our stomachs drop. We paddled closer to the beach and realized there were ten foot waves crashing the shoreline. We had to ride them in to get to the shore.

Neither of us had surfed waves over five feet and that was on a eight foot board. We were on twelve foot paddle boards with gear strapped to the front. Knowing waves come in sets, sometimes three to five bigger waves then a minute or so break of smaller waves then bigger waves again, we waited for the smaller set to roll in. And waited, and waited, patiently, in the pitch black.

Thinking the set had passed, I told Holly that we needed to

hurry while paddling like mad towards the beach. Next thing I know, I hear her screaming "wait", but only for a moment, because then a ginormous wave picked me up and pummeled me, dragging me under the water and into the beach. I was held under longer than I have ever been before. I came up from the dark ocean to the dark sky and all I saw was my best friend kneeling on her board being picked up by the next wave and coming right for my head.

If the board wasn't going to knock me out then the fin would surely cut my head open. I dove under water the best I could, my board still attached to my leg by a leash, and covered my head with my arms to protect myself. Holly's board flipped sideways before it hit me and the ocean took them both for a ride.

The waves hit us again and again, dragging us into the beach and then back out again. Holly was screaming "Shit, Sue" over and over. As another wave took me under I felt myself dragged again by my paddleboard which was still attached to my ankle. Releasing the strap from my ankle, I realize I could stand, and fight the pull of the ocean retuning from the beach.

When I finally made it safely to the beach, I saw Holly standing in the water, fighting not to be dragged back out, still hollering. I ran in the water to grab her. Her board and paddle were gone. She handed me the gear she was clutching and I made my way to shore, thinking she was behind me. I put the gear on the beach and turned to her but found she was still standing in the water, trying to find her board and paddle.

"Leave it," I yelled, trying to grab her and trying to get her to shore. Just as another large set came in, she saw the paddle and grabbed it, but not without immediately getting pummeled by another wave which washed us up to the beach, where our boards- which had also washed up- were waiting for us.

We stood in silence, looking at the ocean, and then at each other, not knowing what to say. One moment I was so happy to be alive and the next I was furious for putting us in this situation. I couldn't stand to be in my own skin. An hour passed and I started in, unable to contain the anxiety.

"I need a moment," Holly interrupted. Another hour went by. "I'm freaking out!" I exclaimed. Though I wasn't even sure what to say, I needed to talk this out, to hear her say she was ok. Holly took her hair conditioner out of the bag and began to comb her hair peacefully and rhythmically in silence, then said "I can't believe I'm going to say this, but I feel much better. Sit down, let's talk."

Though we both were concerned with how we were going to get out past the breakers, never mind make our 8:00 p.m. flight, we decided to enjoy what we could while we where there. We'd lost a lot of gear but still had champagne, cheese and a Twix bar.

Just as she said it would, the full moon, which rose above the cliffs during our makeshift picnic, amped things up. To our right was a group of about forty hippie kids, playing the drums and singing by a campfire. To the left of us was a family that never stopped fighting, both verbally and physically. It was probably the worst I'd ever witnessed. If I could have called the police, I would have.

The good and bad vibes on either side of us seemed to swirl around us throughout the night as Holly and I went from feeling so blessed to be alive and in such a magical place to hashing out all the complexities in our head. "How will we get out?" and "We should have never done this" were compounded with our own personal issues and anxieties. We never went to sleep that night.

At three that morning, the moon lit up the sky and Holly was ready to start our paddle back. I wanted to wait for more light. I was confident in my paddle strength that I could get out but I wasn't feeing confident about Holly. Her shoulders seemed weaker than ever. The wind picks up down the coastline at nine o'clock so we planned on leaving at six, giving us more than enough time to get back before struggling upwind.

We ran though our options: we could paddle back, hike out and leave our boards without shoes or water, or see if one of the locals who took a boat in would give us a ride. I ran down the beach to ask a local. It was eighty dollars on a first-come basis starting at 6am. Our gear was packed. Though I had no money on me, I decided that boating out would be our best and safest option. Holly declined, "We got ourselves into this mess and we are gonna do whatever it takes to get ourselves out."

"Then let me ride your board," I told her. She finally agreed. I packed up Holly's original board with the gear on the front and we waited for the set to pass.

Lucky for us, the waves were only about four feet high. Holly jumped on her board and went for it. I jumped on mine and a wave rushed over my board and slid the gear from the front of my board to my feet. I got washed up on shore, while Holly was waiting for me outside the break. I tightened down the gear and waited for the set to pass, jumped on the board and paddled with all my might to get outside the breaking waves. I struggled but made it, my heart pounding as I stood up to go. But I was not going anywhere. I was paddling but not moving forward at all.

It was the *board*, not Holly's shoulder. This was going to be a long, difficult paddle. We paddled on in silence. The winds came early that morning. We had been paddling for two hours, and the last hour would be against a thirty mph headwind with gusts of forty to forty-five mph. We got on our knees and paddled; it was going slow.

Occasionally a wind gust would last for thirty seconds, stabilizing us or even pushing us backwards. "Just paddle. Hold your ground. Don't get frustrated," I'd holler out, not only for Holly but for myself as well. An hour later we found ourselves in sight of the end. In our exhaustion we somehow made it through the reef unharmed. We got back to the beach and sat in silence. There was nothing to be said, just a deeply amazing appreciation for life.

GIVE BACK: THE KEY TO EVERYDAY SUCCESS

My travels teach me much about myself and what is important to me, but really it's where I choose to live that teaches me the most. My life in Key West is full of ups and down but I have never felt so alive and fulfilled. Besides the business, friends and overall lifestyle, I finally filled in the one missing piece that makes it complete. I gave back.

I have read in every business book about how true wealth lives when you can give back. The capacity in which you give is up to you. I have always been giving of my business knowledge to help others open and grow their own businesses, but it was never enough. A year ago I got involved with our local Special Olympics program. The woman running the program was a paddleboarder and she wanted to bring paddleboarding to the Special Olympics.

I would donate our boards and my time, along with fellow paddlers and friends Holly, Sandy and Trish. Even my dog Casey, who I certified as a therapy dog and service dog, got involved. Each Friday night or Saturday morning we would work with our Special Olympic athletes with various levels of skill, teaching them basic paddleboarding.

Eventually, this group progressed so much that we were training each week instead of just teaching technique. One girl was so inspired by paddling that she lost thirty pounds. Others gained a confidence about them that was life changing. It was the most rewarding experience of my life, and it had nothing to do with me.

Though I had always read about giving back, it wasn't until I became involved that I truly understood the meaning of success. I don't ever want to tell someone they **have** to do something, but I would say giving back is the best way to show your gratitude.

Find something that you are passionate about. If it's not a cause that inspires you, then try an activity that inspires you. Maybe you love art. Work with children who use art as therapy. If you love cooking, maybe donate your time and talent at the local soup kitchen. Find a cause that sparks your heart. I would have told you if I was to get involved in a cause it would be cancer because my aunt died of breast cancer. But instead, my dog and paddleboarding led me to Special Olympics and this is where I feel best invested.

Giving back has nothing to do with money, although if you have some, it always helps. Time is usually your best asset. Your time is valuable to yourself and others. You can donate it and truly make a difference. While money always helps an organization, it most often isn't the same as giving back. You aren't investing in a way that makes the kind of connection I'm talking about. (If you don't have time then reread this book because I addressed many ways to create time).

The biggest personal impact volunteering made on my life is that it got me out of my little world. My life became less significant as far as all the little issues and concerns, helping to create a sense of peacefulness that in turn helps me enjoy every aspect of my life with more ease and comfort.

When you master the art of giving back, please share your story with me (send to the address on the copyright page). Let's make a difference by getting involved and sharing our experiences and motiving others to do the same. The world will be a more peaceful place.

MAKE A DIFFERENCE ON A DAILY BASIS

Even if you have not found your volunteer niche, if you come into contact with people each day then you have the opportunity to make a difference in someone's life. A simple "hello," a smile at a stranger, stopping to talk to someone by actually making the time to see them, sending a quick, friendly text to let that person know you are thinking of them, even just eye contact--all of these things can make a world of difference in someone's day. So often we get caught up in our own days and what we are doing that we don't take the time to see all that is around us.

At Lazy Dog, we are surrounded by people all day. People who chose to spend their hard-earned money and travel to Key West for vacation and then come out to kayak or paddleboard with us or just stop by to grab a tee-shirt. How we treat these people-- our customers-- can make a huge difference in their experience in Key West and at Lazy Dog.

We have the "power" to make a difference. You, me, everyone--we all have this power. By taking the time, by engaging and by making people feel significant, you can put a smile on someone's face and that is a beautiful thing. We are all going though our ups and downs in life and you can make it easier by simply treating people with kindness. Ultimately it will make you feel as good as they do.

When I get emails back from customers or read online TripAdvisor reviews about an experience someone had at Lazy Dog and they say it was the highlight of their vacation it makes me feel like we, as a company, gave back. It is the most rewarding part of the job and completes the picture of success for us.

DO THIS: It's The Little Things That Mean A Lot

Go through your day today and see how many people and in how many different ways you can make someone's day. Be sure to end your day with your gratitude journal and describe your day. You will sleep with a peaceful heart and mind.

THE BOTTOM LINE

If I can leave you with two final words it would be **to live** and living comes through experiencing. It doesn't mean you are great at everything you do, you just have to do it.

Don't worry about being perfect. Don't worry about failing. Just participate in everything. Don't be like most people who don't do things. Be a rarity and live life through experiencing.

Living is about experiences, good or bad. Take them for what they are and realize that is life. The more you live and experience and expand your capacity for living the more you will realize you are alive and this in turn will fuel you to live.

And don't forget that it's the people who make the difference, so embrace those around you, even those you don't know.

Having millions without having the time and people to share it with is not much fun. The true value of life is in your lifestyle and the people with whom you share it.

The literal and figurative wealth of my life continues to surprise me and bring me so much joy, and I can honestly say it's because of a simple code I carry for **really living**:

Engage with people.
Treat people with kindness.
Listen.
Be in one hundred percent.
Have fun.
Laugh.
Don't judge.
Stay open-minded.
Everyone has something to offer and you have
    something for everyone.
Be patient.
Don't be so controlled by time.
Stay in the moment.
Don't waste time thinking about what you've lost.
Stop worrying about the future.
Don't kick yourself when you're down.
Get out of your head.
You don't need stuff.
It's OK to change your mind.
Choose to be happy.

By making these seemingly simple instructions a regular part of who I am and what I do, the Millionaire in Flip Flops lifestyle can't help but continue to find me.

BE HAPPY (THE ALTERNATIVE SUCKS!)

I can share all my stories but ultimately, it's really up to you. It's your choice-- are you going to be happy? I personally recommend being happy because what's the alternative?

Are you going to live where you want to live or not? Are you going to do a job you like or not? Are you going to surround yourself with people you like or not?

Whether it's Key West or some other destination that you consider beautiful and inspiring, find your passion and make it your life's work.

Do whatever it is your heart desires with this short time on this earth. Jump in, get involved, stop procrastinating.

When you follow your heart and stay true to who you are and what you want, it opens the door to an exciting life. *Your life.*

So go. Do it now--make it happen, and by all means, have some fun while you're doing so. The riches of your life are waiting for you.

My Thank Yous.

I am blessed to have so many people who have supported and guided me though my life and have made my Millionaire in Flip Flops lifestyle attainable and that much more enjoyable. **Elisa Levy Green,** for being there for me always with the truth and amazing support. I never would have written this book without your support and guidance. **Robyn Roth,** you have always been a constant, steady support. You are my rock. **Holly Amodio,** for supplying me with the coloring pencils for my life. My world is much more colorful, beautiful and alive thanks to you. Thank you for sharing some of the most amazing adventures of my life. **Peter Green,** a brilliant businessman and wonderful friend. My business guru who has always been there to remind me there are no dead ends, only speed bumps. **Tommy Taylor,** thank you for training my mind and body for the "Olympics of life." **Pat Croce,** for believing in me and helping me step up my game. **Richard and Bethany McColley,** for looking after my dog Casey so I could travel the world. I would have never done that without you both. You are family to me and my trusted and beautiful lifelong friends. **Kathy Gilmour,** my trusted business operations manager for running Lazy Dog and encouraging me so I could travel, write my book and franchise the company. **Dave Richard,** through it all, I choose to remember all the fun we had. **Casey Dog,** my companion. You make my life complete. **Molly Dog,** my old dog that passed away at age 12 of cancer. A soul mate. **Michel Gehin,** for healing my mind and body. You saved me. To my amazing **Lazy Dog staff and extended friends** who make my every day fun. **Cricket Desmarais,** for working with me through all my insecurities and emotions in the completion of this book. I never would have finished it without you.

I'M SO GRATEFUL

ABOUT THE AUTHOR

Sue Cooper is an entrepreneur and owner of Lazy Dog Adventures in Key West, Florida.

Sue spends her time paddleboard racing, working in and building her Lazy Dog business, public speaking, writing and traveling the world with friends while racing and promoting her Lazy Dog brand.

She lives in Key West with her dog Casey, a rescue border collie.

You can follow Sue Cooper at
Sue Cooper on Facebook
Lazy Dog on Facebook
LazyDog.com
MillionaireinFlipFlops.com

Made in the USA
San Bernardino, CA
08 January 2015